The Wisdom of Jacob's Ladder

The Wisdom of Jacob's Ladder

Jacob Cooper

Waterside Productions

ISBN-13: 978-1-958848-80-7 print edition
ISBN-13: 978-1-958848-81-4 e-book edition

Waterside Productions

2055 Oxford Ave
Cardiff, CA 92007
www.waterside.com

To Michael, Grandpa Seymour, Robert, Monty
Mama, Rhonda, Grandpa Paul
and Grandma Florence

"I have arrived, I am home in the here,
in the now. I am solid,
I am free. In the ultimate I dwell."
—Thich Nhat Hanh

Table of Contents

Advance Praise for The Wisdom of Jacobs Ladder

"When I read Jacob Cooper's chapter titled 'The Light at the End of the Ladder,' it became clear to me that the author had not only glimpsed the anticipated light at the end of the tunnel, he had experienced Its infinite radiance and was actively choosing to live in Its service. If you are ready to climb Jacob's ladder of increased understanding and expand your awareness accordingly, you will treasure the gift of this enlightening book."

—Gary E. Schwartz, PhD, Professor of Psychology, Medicine, Neurology, Psychiatry, and Surgery at the University of Arizona and author of *The Afterlife Experiments*, *The G.O.D. Experiments*, and *The Energy Healing Experiments*

"Jacob Cooper's life was profoundly changed forever by an NDE when he was just a boy. Since then, he's been on a soul journey looking for ways to help others to heal and grow. Jacob's genuine and insightful; if you're looking for your own answers in life, his new work *The*

Wisdom of Jacob's Ladder will act as an excellent tour guide on your own personal journey."

—Allison DuBois, inspiration for the hit NBC television show *Medium*, host of the podcast *The Dead Life*, and *New York Times* best-selling author

"Who better to guide you to an understanding of your true Home than a sensitive, loving soul who remembers the lessons learned in his own visit across the veil? Jacob has packed this treasure of a book with spiritual truths and practical tools delivered with his signature compassion and hard-earned wisdom. Read it and remember!"

—Suzanne Giesemann, author of *Messages of Hope* and founder of The Awakened Way™.

"I call life a mysterious miracle. So read on and enjoy your potential. When the truth is shared, we all begin to experience life as it truly is. Well done."

—Bernie Siegel, MD, *New York Times* best-selling author of *Love, Medicine & Miracles* and *The Art of Healing*

"Jacob Cooper is a dynamic thought leader. His hard-earned wisdom and connection to spirit shines through this book. *The Wisdom of Jacob's Ladder* is an engaging read that includes deep and practical wisdom from higher awareness."

—Kimberly Meredith, Medical Intuitive, best-selling author *Awakening to the Fifth Dimension: Discovering the Soul's Path to Healing*

"Jacob Cooper has written a genuinely uplifting, healing work that reassures us that we don't die. After having an NDE when he was three years old, Jacob realized that our time on earth is all about love. Jacob's book, filled with practical advice for living a more fulfilled life, is especially significant to anyone who has experienced the passing of a loved one. Knowing, as Jacob does, that they are happy, healthy, and whole allows us to move forward and heal. Thank you, Jacob, for this beautiful work."

—Elizabeth Boisson, President and Cofounder of Helping Parents Heal

"Jacob Cooper deeply inspires in a voice that is genuine and calming. He gently guides the seeker to shift from thoughts that have self-destructive power as well as potential to harm others. He makes becoming more conscious feel not only easy, but natural and comforting. His empathic, intelligent book opens both the heart and mind in a harmonious work that adds more love and understanding to a world in great need of it."

—Elaine Clayton, author of *The Way of the Empath* and *Making Marks: Discover the Art of Intuitive Drawing*

"Jacob Cooper, LCSW, is a dynamic up-and-coming star who I have been privileged to interview on my program. This book reflects hard-earned wisdom through Jacob's profound near-death experience and subsequent encounters. A truly enlightening and meaningful read."

—George Noory, Host of the national radio show *Coast to Coast AM*

"Jacob's life and service to others is a great example of how near-death experiencers can provide much hope and power to others. I highly recommend *The Wisdom of Jacob's Ladder* to help lighten and enlighten your earthly experience. You don't have to nearly die to remember the big picture of life and live accordingly. This book will show you how."

—Mark Pitstick, MA, DC, SoulProof.com, SoulPhone.com, GreaterRealityLiving.com

"Jacob Cooper's book *The Wisdom of Jacob's Ladder* provides a guide to finding different ways to view and live life. Cooper mixes his deep spirituality as well as his knowledge of human psychology as he looks at people as sacred beings who are engaging, experiencing, and responding to everyday life. He asserts that we are not 'doing' but 'being.' In line with this thought, he astutely defines the word 'wisdom' as a higher awareness in our everyday lives; wisdom is not seen as something that we learn outside of ourselves but rather it is a part of our natural instinct to who we are and how we see life. He espouses the idea that we do not have to wait until our physical bodies die (because he attests that our souls live on) to feel joy and a connection to God, but rather we can feel it while we are alive. Cooper says that we do not have to wait until we die to feel full of life, but rather to feel it while we walk this earth. He contends that 'being truly alive is awakening from the dream of being separate from the light on the other side and connecting to it in all that we do.' *The Wisdom of Jacob's Ladder* is a wonderful book that teaches people how to see the sacred inside themselves and truly live their lives though open eyes."

—Anna L. Raimondi, *Conversations with Mary*, (Simon & Schuster, 2017)

"The after gifts of near-death experiences often produce wisdom. Jacob Cooper has spent his interior, intellectual, and professional life pursuing the noetic knowledge gifted to him in his NDE. His book *The*

Wisdom of Jacob's Ladder abounds with insightful handholds and footings for those on the ascent."

—Peter Panagore, MDiv., author of the Audible international best seller *Heaven Is Beautiful*

"An excellent resource and guide for those trying to enhance their spirituality within their lives."

—Jeffrey A. Wands, Internationally acclaimed Psychic Medium and author of *Another Door Opens*

"After reading Jacob Cooper's book, it was clear to me that in his innocence of experiencing an NDE that he brought back the gift of universal truths that would otherwise have taken many lifetimes to discover. This book is a life changer and will help guide you in your own soul's journey."

—Josephine Ghiringhelli, Psychic Medium, President and Founder of Metaphysical Alternatives, Public Speaker, and Intuitive Counselor

"*The Wisdom of Jacob's Ladder* is an engaging, educational, and excellent read. Like the account of Jacob's Ladder in the book of Genesis, this book poses many questions about the connection between life and the afterlife. Drawing upon his childhood near-death experience in harmony with his work as a therapist, meticulous research, and his own sensitive and introspective nature, Cooper demystifies and removes the fear of the unknown we call death. *The Wisdom of Jacob's Ladder* presents valuable and practical insights on understanding life in this world, and the one yet to come."

—Mark Anthony, JD, best-selling author of *The Afterlife Frequency, Never Letting Go* and *Evidence of Eternity*

Foreword

Since the dawn of man, we mortals have been contemplating two big questions. Either consciously or subconsciously, we want to know if there is any meaning or purpose to physical life and if we go somewhere else when the ride is over. Some of us form opinions about these questions based upon outside influences such as our religion, educators, families, media, societal norms, or science. Others tend to go within to find such answers as they search for a pathway to connect to sources that transcend the physical experience.

Many near-death experiencers such as Jacob Cooper are blessed with insights that usually remain hidden to those immersed in the trials and tribulations of physical life. Too many of us live our lives as isolated entities and fear the finality of death. It can be debilitating to our mental and physical health and cause us to miss the true purpose of life. It is only when we surrender to a greater force, to fields of connectiveness, that we can evolve and thrive. The metaphorical ladder described in this book is a progression from vague hope, to belief, to knowing. The knowing stage is transformative and comes with the realization that we are far more than our physical bodies, there is order behind the chaos, and physical life is an experience from which we grow.

When a loved one dies, it is easy to say that death is only an illusion, but quite a different story knowing it on a soul level. We grieve because we love, and the pain of not being able to hold them in the physical can be devastating. So how does one reach the point of recognizing that not only do they still exist, but they retain their memories and personality? One way, as described by Jacob, is to simply surrender to unseen forces that envelop us. We need to stop reasoning and judging and start experiencing. In my own case, I was caught up in materialist left-brain thinking, and that prevented me from recognizing the signs and connectivity that were all around me. I needed science and evidence to flip my thinking, but people like Jacob and others with spiritual knowledge do not need such reinforcement.

Having a profound nonphysical experience like an NDE is certainly a shortcut to the recognition that we reside in a continuum of life, but there are other ways. Altered states of consciousness are conducive to receiving such knowledge, and those can be obtained by quieting our minds. Meditation, being immersed in nature, music, or art are pathways to the mystical. Dream visitations and after-death communications can have profound effects on grief and the way we think about death.

I am grateful for people like Jacob Cooper who remind me to let go of restrictive thoughts and open my mind to the infinite universe. It sounds so easy, but it is exceedingly difficult to simply breathe and allow yourself to live. We have been put on this earth to experience, and it is as simple as that. We evolve in the realms that await us, but how we face our earthly travails may very well chart our course to enlightenment.

Robert Ginsberg
Cofounder of the Forever Family Foundation and author of *The Medium Explosion*

INTRODUCTION

My life changed forever on a warm September morning in 1993. I was just three years old and was going to a playground with family and some friends. When I ran happily toward the playground that day, I had unknowingly contracted pertussis, otherwise known as whooping cough, a contagious and dangerous virus. If left untreated for infants, children, or even adults, it can lead to serious physical damage, and, in my case and many others', passing on.

I climbed the rungs of a ladder toward the top of a slide. Suddenly, I wasn't able to breathe. I began to lose all control over my bodily functions. I was struck with intense panic, trauma, and felt powerless over my own physical demise and despair.

My body was no longer able to function, and yet part of me was able to go on. I stepped out of my body, or "vehicle" as I call it, and began to become aware of my own body and its functions, and I had a clear understanding that all made sense. I was able to see the physical through a much deeper lens of awareness.

I last became aware that my brain was being deprived of oxygen. Moments later, I felt a gigantic crack, like the sound that you hear when thunder strikes. My brain felt as if it literally split in half. I then was able to let go of what felt like an eternity of panic, pain due to my suffocation, and uncertainty. I surrendered to the light of what many know as the higher spirit realm or what is commonly referred to as the other side.

It was an experience that had the intensification of the highest of highs. I became fully aware of the source of all there is and was, otherwise referred to by many as God, awareness of Christ consciousness, angels, spirit guides, soul family, past lives, and my own soul's purpose and more to describe to put properly into words. Later, I learned that this was called a near-death experience (NDE). The term was coined by a world-renowned and brilliant pioneer named Dr. Raymond Moody. My NDE took me to a place that was foreign to my life as a three-year-old to some degree but was near and dear to my own soul.

I became aware of the power of choice. Many NDE-ers report having autonomy over if they stay on the other side or that it is not their time. Within this choice, I became aware of some of the work that I would be doing in my current life and the lives impacted by it. I was very moved and had a clear knowing of what to do.

I chose to continue my mission to help people remember who they are and where they come from. I knew in those moments that I would be a gentle reminder to others of who they are on this earth temporarily but not of it. There was a higher intelligence and infinite source weaving through life, no matter how much one forgot on the journey or little they saw or heard from these unseen force fields of higher awareness.

I wrote my last book *Life After Breath* as a way to give back what I was given. You see, in moments when I experienced the most intensified despair and had my own breath taken, I was able to surrender to the breath of eternity. In the Jewish faith that I was raised in, spirit is translated as *Ruach*, or "Wind of God." This is one of the few points that I have grown to accept and agree within the faith.

I knew that despite losing my own breath, there was a breath that can never be taken from my soul. *Life After Breath* to me was my story or karma of my near-death experience and how I was able to take ownership of it in my life.

I decided to write *The Wisdom of Jacob's Ladder* for many different reasons. The first reason is that while I believe that we all have a story or a karma, we also have the ability to not be defined by our stories. We can learn to define them and create a meaning and purpose. The narrative of my own near-death experience never changed. As I grew and evolved as a human and soul, I was able to find ways to express it and learn from it differently.

I believe life is like a canvas. Each and every day we have the opportunity to create a different outlook and viewpoint. Perception and our awareness of it becomes our reality. *The Wisdom of Jacob's Ladder* is a book that goes into the beautiful tapestry and wisdom that I have been able to learn from my near-death experience.

Plenty of people wait for life to "begin to happen." Some wait consciously or unconsciously to experience bliss when they leave this earth. This book shares that there is no death of the soul in its truest state, despite the death of the body. Plenty fear losing their body enough that at times they forget to live. After my NDE I knew that there was no death; only life could exist.

I decided to live a life dedicated to giving back what I was given. In moments when I felt lifeless, I was given back life. I decided from the ground up in the mental, emotional, psychological, and spiritual standpoint to try to assist others. I often tell my clients that I do not have a magic wand in my pocket. They are capable, resilient, and have a brilliant light that is there deep down that we are here to explore, find, and know.

In my private practice as a clinical social worker, certified hypnotherapist, and Reiki practitioner, I have worked with thousands of individuals. Publicly, I've facilitated events where many are waking up to wanting to live while they are alive. Some of my clients and people I interact with, however, feel as if death is not something that happens to them when they die but rather a state that they are experiencing while they are alive. That being alive is the furthest from them.

In my psychotherapy practice, I have come to value what is referred to as exposure therapy. This is a modality that works in a paradoxical manner. For example, a person may say they fear planes. We don't just avoid that thought. Together, we work on eventually, gradually building the ability to face it head-on. We recognize that where our greatest fears lay is the key to our greatest power.

It is not through avoidance that resolves, but rather approaching it in a safe and supportive therapeutic environment. This helps shape different neuro-interpretations of the phobia, fear, or comorbid mental health condition past a block. I often contemplate to myself how to utilize exposure therapy through death. I would most definitely lose my license and most certainly be pressed with intense charges if I set clients up in a self-induced lab to have near-death experiences through direct exposure.

But through gradual exposure, I have found that by talking about it and finding different interpretations from the ground up all the way through hearing it from a therapist who works with clients on these modalities but someone who has had a near-death experience himself puts me in a unique category and vantage point to change others' conditions surrounding death.

This book helps in this regard from the ground up in recognizing death as part of our human journey, but not the full picture or the totality of it. In other words, death is an experience, but there is a life that can go on for the loved one who passed as well as having permission within our own lives here on earth and discovering our own way to continue to live.

It has been a difficult time to live on this planet for many. The COVID-19 pandemic continues to impact our lives. Over the last few years, there have been horrifying spikes in gun violence and political divides happening here in my native country and throughout many parts of the world. The current war in Ukraine and mass global unrest have created a lot of uncertainty and devastation for many. It seems as if the world we are living in is creating our state of mind and not the other way around. While there are certainly many problems, I believe that wisdom is the oxygen of our times. Albert Einstein once famously stated that we cannot solve our problems with the same thinking we used when we created them. While we are not responsible for creating this mess, we are dependent on finding alternative ways of living and viewing the problem to get ourselves out of it. When we change our outlook and tap into a higher gear, one person's life at a time will shift.

With this book, I am here to make a change. I invite you to come with me on a story-based transformative experience in my near-death experience. It is a catalyst for our times. It is a resilient piece in having a different set of sources running and governing our lives. This is not sourced in ego, division, or the narratives played out in our worlds. It is a source that goes far beyond this. A source that never left our own backyard of our inner being. At our core and deepest essence, we are this source and solution to everyday problems.

Plenty of clients and people I interact with on a daily basis search for happiness and God, turning away from their own source within and looking thousands of miles away. It's as if the notion that we are not good enough has governed lives and answers, with beauty and wisdom coming from something else.

I learned in my NDE that all one has to do is turn inward and change their direction. To let go of the pain and suffering that exists temporarily in the body and human condition and embrace one's true foundation of source of life. I learned that our thoughts, emotions, and states come and go as well as even the pain and suffering. I am living proof through my own NDE. What lasts is the soul. How we remember our soul can lead to the life that we live and the ability to nurture and embody our essence.

On the following pages, I have divided different lessons into different chapters. I had my own NDE on a ladder, like Jacob from the Bible who saw angels floating up and down after fleeing from his brother Esau. This book provides different tenets and wisdom of each rung of the ladder. Upon applying to some of these tenets, one can begin to remind themselves that they do not have to wait to get to heaven to see the light that this light, this inner light, never left them.

Every step in our experience is focused on our own true being, not the doing of the world, which changes temporarily. Being presence with each step on the ladder of growth, expansion, and guidance can assist seekers reading this book to remember that they are all spiritual beings not defined by this human experience but here and able to define and share this human experience.

I have included in chapters a few impactful guided meditations that can assist in bringing forward higher awareness. Many people in my workshops and book signings have asked to have self-induced near-death experiences. I tell them politely that it sounds good having one, but you do not have to die to experience awareness of your soul and all the love that connects you in the heavens and earth.

You can safely practice going inward or what is commonly known as mediation. In this practice you become aware of a timeless time and spaceless space. You get into the silence that you know you can't cut up, measure, or size down. When you are truly connected, you are not the thinker, the emotions, the body, the ego, or the labels of this life that you are playing out but rather simply the eternal observer.

I included meditation and segments to assist others going inward in this book as it's a major rung of the ladder to experience similar awareness of the higher mind that I had in my NDE without needing the extensive trauma of suffocation.

I learned in my NDE that once I was able to surrender to a light, I was able to step into an awareness that saved my suffering.

In my experience, letting go and accepting the wisdom of the other side has been a saving grace. In moments when I felt stuck, uncertain, or afraid that the darkness outside of myself would overtake my own inner happiness, I was able to let go and find the answers. *The Wisdom of Jacob's Ladder* does not intend to solve the outer experiences and justifications of the world that we are experiencing today.

Rather, this is a book that acts as a guide to finding different ways to pivot, engage, and respond to our everyday events. I have come to realize that life has very little to do with what is actually happening in front of us. The majority of it is based on interpretation and the foundation that I respond. I use the term "wisdom" as the more we apply higher awareness in our everyday lives; wisdom is not seen as an idea that we learn outside of ourselves but rather it becomes the fila and fabric of our natural instinct to who we are and how we see life.

Now is a time of needed repair. I believe that war and peace are based on our connection to source. When we are connected to peace and fully embrace it as our true nature, the war that we live with becomes a foreign practice and ceases to exist. In other words, as stated earlier, do not hold your breath for yourself to see a light in waiting for the world to change. It starts within each person to change the world. You and I, we are our world.

While writing this book, I had a near and dear grandmother who passed away at a ripe age. Of course, I would love to hold on to her here physically on this earth, but I know that she is with me. I included a chapter in my own book on different ways to utilize afterlife awareness as a tool to assist with grief. I bring her up to conclude this introduction. She would end every call with, "Jake, take care of precious you." It became so routine to hear that it that it almost lost its value.

I know she was pivotal in writing this book. In her last days she would keep a copy of my first book by her and smile at it each time I visited her. When I told her the name of this book, she replied in a joking way, "The Wisdom of Jacob's Bladder." I laughed hysterically, because no matter how much pain she had, her own joy and laughter were her guide and true source of life no matter what occurred.

I may have to write an entire series on The Wisdom of Jacob's Bladder, I told her, but it would take countless bathroom breaks that might interfere with the process.

I carry her message with me in this book, as at times we can forget that we are precious. Life can override our identity, make no mistake about it; the world can be a cruel place. I ask as you read this book to always remember that no matter what happens, there is a sacred beauty in each and every one of you. You come from the divine and are forever connected to it.

Michelangelo was once asked how he created his masterpieces. He would respond, "I just chip away at the masterpiece within." We all have this masterpiece within, but we have falsely learned that it has to be something like a job, a state in our lives, or a constant checklist to "be" something. Be still and remember this: you are a sacred being, not a "doing" but a "being." You are more than you can ever imagine. Enjoy the steps on the ladder as I take you on a familiar journey and awareness that we are all forever connected to.

Make sure to not only read this book. Live it. Apply it. Know it and you will see those God winks that remind us that heaven never left us. It is right here. Right now, in this very moment.

Chapter One: Re-Remembering Your Nature

After all, we're just walking each other home.
—Ram Dass

Returning with descriptive information after a journey to the other side has been a daunting challenge. It was difficult to put words to the seemingly infinite place without applications of earthly time, space, color, or sounds. After all, I was only three years old at the time. I had barely figured out the basics of this world, and in one moment I found myself on the other side thanks to a fall from a tall slide at the park. Can you imagine what that was like, growing up coming back from something like that so young?

My near-death experience involves another realm and even another language. This is the crux of what has held me back in many aspects of this life for almost twenty years. The clumsy communication method of the spoken word here is seemingly pointless when discussing the other side. Knowing the reality—or rather, unreality—of death, I have been blessed and touched as a psychotherapist, even within my own personal times of grief.

I've grappled with the purpose and steps of emotionally processing loss from this human side while also keeping in mind the illusion of loss in the first place, having a recollection of the purely comical nature of the term "loss" when describing the seeming "ending" of a loved one. I now look at life and death as one and the same.

When we look back on our lives, within an ending, there is grief but also a new beginning. Within a new beginning, there is still grief but also the excitement of a rebirth. I have experienced this as being no different within our physical lives. In bodily death, there is a rebirth of the spirit in its infinite awareness without physical limitations.

Well-chronicled near-death experience researcher P. M. H. Atwater discusses that childhood near-death experiencers take on average around thirty years to fully integrate and process their experience. In her groundbreaking book on extensive research on children NDE's, Atwater (2019) discusses that children NDE's "compensate, adjust and ignore but according to what I've seen do not even begin the integration process until somewhere between twenty to forty years of age: 'Yes many of them imprint or bond to the other side.' But, and it's a big but, the job of any child in society is to learn and grow. Anything that interferes with that job is tucked away, ignored, or forgotten. Sometimes the only way child experiencers can be recognized is the pattern of aftereffects they display... without knowing why" (P.

M. H. Atwater, 2019, p. 144). As I write this, it has been nearly twenty-seven years since my own near-death experience in September 1993. Every day I challenge myself on a personal and professional level to describe what I saw and make sense out of it.

This endeavor involves breaking it into language fitting for a dimension outside of the various belief systems that others dearly hold in their consciousnesses. If you look back at world explorers, they dared to challenge themselves to go to the other side of the world to disprove the world was flat. Similarly, the spies of the Judea tribes went to the Land of Israel to make a descriptive report, but it was challenging to place words on what was viewed.

After getting in touch with the other side and the infinite, I found that not only was there no time but there was no space. Eternity was a mind-boggling concept and construct compared to the linear time and spatial dimensions that I was programmed to. Wisdom can be gained within eternity, but to understand its language, one has to process it with a source comparable to it.

Just as it would be quite difficult to have a conversation with a whale, it is difficult to conceptualize the fabric of the eternity of the soul with a mind that operates in linear terms. A helpful tool to better acclimate and bring forward the experience is getting in touch with the sacred silence within all of us, or what some refer to as meditation. Through meditation, I am not only able to make sense of my NDE but am also able to go back to it. Meditation is the best way for others to experience a sense of timelessness and infinity with no beginning, middle, or end. The only thing getting in the way of perception of the endless sacred silence within is the editing commentary of the analytical mind.

One of the most significant messages and invaluable lessons from my experience was making sense of the infinite. In addition, my experience posed the question of why I had this double-edged sword of a near-death experience that traumatized my body through suffocation but invigorated my soul at such a young age.

One possible answer was within the symmetry of destiny of my name: Jacob. I don't think it was a coincidence that my parents gave me this name. Jacob from the Bible had a dream in which he ascended a ladder from the earthly realm to the heavenly realm then returned back down. The dream made it clear to him that his life's purpose was to lead the Israelites and grow their nation. I had my own experience, not within the dream state but by having my own body give out on me. Like the biblical Jacob, I glimpsed the ultimate freedom and knowledge of home. After coming up each step of the ladder, it was on the final rung that I ascended into heaven and came down with information from each rung that was stepped on.

When I give public workshops and lectures, the most commonly asked questions are related to who I am, why I'm here, and what my purpose is. After noticing this pattern, I am prepared to answer by first asking others to point to who they are. In response, the majority of audience members will point to their hearts, their solar plexus, or other parts of their body.

I then ask a follow-up question of why they didn't point to their car in the parking lot or their homes in the neighborhood. They often give me a perplexed look.

"Why not?" I will inquire next.

They reply, "My car isn't me, and neither is my home."

I then ask them to explain their reason, but they are not sure.

"So, why did you point to your body? What is the difference? Much like you are not your car, home, and bank account, are you your body?"

They say, "I see myself that way in the mirror."

I explain how we define ourselves by how we see ourselves. Like the car or the house, the body is a mechanism that gets us from point A to point B in our lives, but we weren't born from it, nor can we take it with us when we are gone. So then, what are we?

When I was just three years old, I learned that the soul was not produced by my body or defined by my body. Within my near-death experience, my soul was felt most distinctly when the brain and the physical body shut down due to lack of oxygen. I discovered that I was sustained by the eternal breath of infinite spirit. My soul passed through a portal to a familiar place, a place of great comfort, love, and sensation that I struggled to put into words.

Once I recognized that I was not my body, everything changed. I was able to awaken from the slow slumber of the material world that was beginning to falsify my identity toward knowing that these were merely forms that I could utilize to bring forward a true purpose in this world. What is that purpose, I am asked. Why did I come down to this world? Was it to pay the bills, deal with difficult family members, and overcome earthly challenges?

I am often perplexed by this question regarding life's purpose. It was answered within my own experience as a young boy by remembering the charting phase of my soul prior to my human life. Much like Jacob from the Bible, I remembered a sense of challenges laid out before me. Some of these challenges (which I will get into later in this book) were living out the allegorical reference of the light at the end of the tunnel in my near-death experience and overcoming a fear of being stuck.

In a prior incarnation, I was unable to accomplish this task and ended up taking my own life for this reason. My purpose now was to have faith in my knowing. Another purpose was to find a blessing in my despair and suffocation, to be a harbinger of good news that a rebirth and even euphoria is available not only at the end of our lives but at any time. This state of heightened experience underlines who we truly are as high vibratory spiritual beings who do not have to be held captive and programmed by the material world.

A shift to knowing starts in a simple way that is often overlooked. Many times, I share with others how the majority of us, from an early age, are spoken of as our bodies and not as our souls. We are treated as if there is nothing more to our nature, so we take on that ideology and forget. The greatest sin we can have, in my experience, is to forget who we are and become something and someone else. Then we are conditioned to act on what we are perceived to be, eventually having that false belief ingrained within our identity.

It is no surprise that when asked to define themselves, most people point at their bodies because that is what they were taught they are. I had to lose control of my body to gain awareness that I was much more. It is also not a surprise that people commonly ask about their purpose because they have many times lost touch with their true nature, their soul, and its infinite wisdom to guide them in their lives.

When it comes to life's purpose, the biggest challenge for others as a collective is to be able to shed the identity and level of consciousness that was inherited in years prior and come back home. I call it a re-remembering and reunification of coming from home.

Throughout my experience as a teacher, I have noticed that so many people are feeling bogged down and depressed. I wonder why that is, but I find that this lifetime can be challenging when many of us are inherently stuck in the material and the body. We confine and limit ourselves as highly vibratory free beings. On a daily basis, our worldview is portrayed with displays of discord, wars, and poverty as our true identity. Yet, many who are waking up have all the checkmarks on the pedestal of human existence—cars, partners, jobs, and picture-perfect families—but something is profoundly missing.

The part that many people are feeding to itch and can't quite put into words is a bogged-down soul. I lived this for many years during most of my childhood and young adulthood. Particularly between the childhood and adolescent angst I desperately tried to keep up with the rat race and the world's speed in front of me. I neglected and buried that deep, mystical part for many years, so I fully understand the struggle.

We are taught to feed our brains in school through regurgitation. Then we feed our bodies and egos through competition and bank accounts. Having more of these externals that we identify ourselves with is perceived as success. I often sense the deeper hunger that people have. This comes from the soul with its need of nourishment. The soul needs to feed its internal nature and find deeper satisfaction outside of fleeting material, linear constructs.

Many times, people are looking for happiness in all the wrong places. The material world constantly teaches us to feed a machine with a temporary nature. People get burned out by trying to satiate something that was never meant to be satiated. I link it to going to the arcade and playing Whac-A-Mole. The addictive impulses and drive to feed never ends, just like the Buddhist concept of the hungry ghost.

According to Dr. Gabor Maté, renowned specialist in anxiety and addiction, the "difference between passion and addiction is that between a divine spark and a flame that incinerates." Only when one gets in touch with one's soul do they recognize that less is more. When one realizes that the beginning, the end, and the alpha and omega of the soul's nature and destiny is love, there are less superfluous thoughts, fewer meaningless drives to acquire, and no more frenzied neediness for validation. No additional muscle or routes are needed to gain self-approval or love.

The struggle to find the divine spark of the soul isn't life's purpose. All we need to do is remember our infinite nature and be empowered to listen to it in a world that many times ignores the depths and focuses on the surface. Seeing something that is not physically right in front of us is a challenge for many.

I look at it this way: when we think of faith, we envision the allegorical darkness in the tunnel and trust that there is light at the end of such darkness. Why is it that some have a hard time with this soul-level faith? Where have we gone awry? To me, the answer is that we were taught to have faith in the finite body and a material world where we have experienced situations where what can go wrong will.

This becomes our frame of reference rather than something infinite that cannot be put into words or touched. Many have taken on this identity of the world with its lack of faith and added to it their own identification with the physical, effectively putting their hands before their eyes and blocking any glimmer or light of hope.

The biggest struggle that I find others have when getting in touch with their soul and the possibility of the infinite is that so many have become accustomed to pain in this world. In fact, a lot of people almost find comfort in its familiarity. This sabotages access to something greater than pain and suffering. Although there are difficult occasions and circumstances, some affecting us deeply, there is always the opportunity to let go of these stories and frameworks to reach toward a higher light, power, and sensation.

Similarly, within a Past Life Regression workshop that I facilitated (this will be explained a little later too), the clients who struggled the most were those who were afraid of letting go and allowing themselves to expand in consciousness. I think this explains the culture of pain that I see as a psychotherapist practicing in the field for several years.

Clients normalize their identity as synonymous with a depressed, anxious, fearful person. They don't define themselves by just the physical body, but also a flawed emotional state. Just as we are conditioned to identify with our physical bodies, when we feed our identification with an emotionally unhealthy pattern, our very selves are given another framework of limitation.

I often ask clients, "When you came into this world as a child, were you depressed, anxious, and angry?" Most of them will stumble with a response or intellectualize and rationalize an excuse to protect themselves. No one can honestly claim to have been depressed, anxious, and angry at birth. I then ask, "So what happened in between?"

The most challenging element that I had within my near-death experience was the willingness to lose myself. By that, I mean in order to cross over to go to the other side, I had to let go of the way that I saw myself—as three-year-old Jake—within that moment of bodily suffocation. Once this happened, a whole new level of infinite grace, wisdom, and guidance was available.

I was able to access the door of the heavenly dimension by letting go of the identity of the door and room of the place I thought I was living in. For many, to get in touch with their soul, life's purpose, and an identity unclouded by fear and limitation, they have to let go of their previously constructed identity and shell. This is often termed "An Awakening." I believe that we are all purely woken, aware beings by nature.

As psychologist Carl Jung wrote: "One who looks outside, dreams. One who looks inside, awakens." This waking up to our true nature is not like sleeping unencumbered in dreams, but it can be likened to the freshness and clarity of waking up in the morning. When the soul is hindered by conditioning and the framework of this physical world, waking up in the morning is basically going back to sleep.

A good example from my own life is how I was overweight in my youth. Because I continually catered to and was fed the identity of a fat child, that was my set perception of "me." We are not only what we eat. We are also what we feed our identities. Much like you wouldn't feed yourself air for breakfast because it wouldn't do a thing for your stomach, you wouldn't feed yourself anything that does not sustain your personal identity and its requirements. Just as I lost weight by recognizing I was not a fat person but happened to be feeding that self-identity, people can change much in their lives by perceiving they are not finite beings.

How then does one magically understand that he or she is infinite? Like I said earlier, it is hard to see the Light when we have our hands in front of our faces blocking it.

So many of us shield and do not listen to Light because we have learned to trust in the physical more so than not. There are constant nudges and voices whispering to us from the other side, but so many of us doubt those love letters of guidance from a loved one on the other side.

Instead, we dismiss them as passing thoughts. As I said before, the brain is merely a filter between the two worlds. I experienced this. I would not recommend depriving yourself of oxygen to get enlightenment—quite the opposite. When we are breathing deeply and calmly, filling the brain and body with more oxygen and connection to the sacred silence within, our brain reaches those deeper brain wave states where we receive messages, many without words.

So many messages are examples of the language of the soul—that nudge to call a friend out of the blue who you ignore only to find out something happened to them days later, or you think of someone whom you haven't spoken with in a long time and within minutes they give you a call. These types of "random encounters" that have happened to us all do not seem random anymore after we begin listening and tuning in to our souls rather than ignoring or bogging down the interplay of guidance in our lives.

One of the most helpful ways to get in touch with the soul and to be guided is to get quiet. This is commonly referred to as meditation, but whatever descriptive language you choose is unimportant and can vary from individual to individual. Many people put the soul on a remote pedestal and dramatize that reaching it is harder than it really is.

I once heard a beautiful saying that prayer is talking to God, and meditation is merely listening. I would like to have you find a practice. Close your eyes for a minute, and do the best you can to not be your thoughts or impulses but rather the observer of what you experience. Can you imagine a reality when that observer of life is not present? It is impossible. That observer in the depths of the ocean is your soul!

I experienced this in my near-death experience. I did not magically change my identity within my experience. The observer was the same. The only thing that shifted was the beauty and grace before me in the heavenly dimension. The soul with its ageless personality, wisdom, and grace is you. This carries no gender, form, or box but is merely a spark of divinity.

Have you ever found that when you have something worrying you and clouding your mind, someone else can be speaking to you, even about something very profound, but you are out of sync with their words? The truth is you are not really there. Often, when people have a hard time meditating or getting in touch with their soul, it is for one of a few reasons. One is they would rather hold on to the belief that there is no soul and continue to be "right" in their own minds than step into meditation and its benefits. Others cling to the many thoughts on their minds and do not quiet them, which limits their ability to go deeper. Others are afraid of letting go of their pain and discomfort and would rather remain in an unhealthy comfort zone.

The Zen form of meditation, commonly portrayed in yoga classes or the massage therapy room, is rooted in Buddhist principles, but meditation does not necessarily need a label. While identifications and developed guidelines of practices can be helpful, I find the most important guideline is finding something that works for each person.

Having crossed over to heaven and seen the Light as a child, I continued to have spiritually transformative experiences. I did not need to go to a formal training program or school to achieve them. The best way to experience what I did is to recognize that formal steps are not needed. You are the holder of the keys of your own soul and the gateway to it. It does not belong to a place that gets your hard-earned money and time. You cannot box in the soul and its connection to the Light. Religions, philosophies, and schools of thought are prisms and pathways up to the mountain of the Light, but they are not the Light. I learned that the best way to understand the soul is to see it as pure Light.

Once a person sees themselves as divine and within Light, everything changes. Regarding meditation, I find that people do not need to go to fancy retreats, although they can if they feel drawn to. The practice can begin with a few moments to themselves. Within their lives, they can recognize that each person, place, and moment is a monastery. Their job is to be able to be a keeper of this Light and to take care of it.

If you owned a bright, brand-new Lamborghini and it got muddy, what would you do? Most would freak out. The same applies once we see ourselves as Light. Darkness and negativity are not as easily tolerable. We sense how they dirty the soul. Inner knowing gives us a higher motive on a daily basis to cleanse the negativity and lift the heaviness from our own Light. Just as a model will watch her diet and carefully monitor her physical state for its identity with beauty and grace, it is the same for individuals who take sacred pride in their souls. There is a great value in maintaining and growing our inner beauty.

Another great way to improve quiet is to get in touch with nature. Nature has allowed me to see a reflection of my own nature from having my out-of-body experience years after my own near-death experience. In the past, I commonly intellectualized with and utilized New Age jargon such as "we are one" with each other and nature. Until I had this experience, I did not know what it meant.

I have learned that inner practice is not about blind faith in fantasy gained from someone else but rather taking away barriers. Realizing oneness involves letting go and having what you experience in your inner world become a form of knowing based on direct experience. Nature is a great way to expand your breath. You can see yourself unfolding into oneness, recognizing the reciprocal dynamic and dependency that you have through breathing in and breathing out.

When others do not nurture their own nature, it leads to nature not being nurtured. The sheer understanding that the planet and humanity on a physiological basis are dependent on each other and in a reciprocal dynamic is vital to the respect, dignity, and grace with which we treat nature and each other. When Mother Earth is taken care of, so are we, and vice versa.

A big question that I have to face through many workshops and lectures is the value of my experience in connecting to infinity and the knowing of the infinite. This awareness was a gift and a challenge that was not easy to grow up with. It was daunting to feel awake in a world that was sleeping. I had a hard time and fell asleep myself for a bit but eventually woke up. On a human level, it is easy to be a leaf in water with the rest. It is more difficult like Abraham from the Bible to be on one side of the river when others are on another.

One of the biggest forms of assistance that I gained through infinite understanding was the power of focusing on what would last and what would be a fleeting thought in time. Having a recollection of infinity, including my past lives and their lessons, allowed me to detach from the material world, recognizing it as one big illusion and temporary dwelling. I viewed that life and all the struggles were a game that I had charted with my guides and others.

I see how some get caught in the game of life and forget the playbook and preparation, reverting to the primitive tendencies within the game. When I remember eternity and my purpose, put more power in knowing, and transform fear into faith (which I did not do in my last life when I took my own life), I am able to utilize this awareness to navigate the difficult times.

Even if one does not believe in eternity, a solid foundation for progress in life through the resilient psychological model is learning to see things in the broader perspective, always understanding that both good and bad moments pass. Resilience theory suggests that it is not adversity that defines us but rather how we define the obstacles. We can all find a way to embrace challenges and allow them to strengthen us as individuals, leading to evolution and triumph.

From this, considering how we come from the loving, wise source of the infinite, the finite planet can be changed. From my experience of temporarily losing my body, I learned there is a tremendous value when we become a game changer and not just a player. I realized that the game plan was made long before me with my guides and soul family. The execution of that plan will hopefully have a ripple effect long after I leave the physical.

Chapter Two: The Illusion of Loneliness

But the greatest suffering is being ***lonely****, feeling unloved, having no one. I have come more and more to realize that it is being unwanted that is the worst disease that any human being can ever experience. There is a terrible hunger for love. We all experience that in our lives—the pain, the* ***loneliness****.*

—Mother Teresa

Throughout time, in one way or another, nearly everyone has felt a sense of isolation, separation, and dread of feeling alone in our pain and suffering. Even with our busy lives, we have family and friends who we know are there for us when need be. What is often found is that others can support and help us, but loneliness is a state of mind that can exist not because of a lack of support but despite it.

One can feel alone even with the support of family and friends when there is lack of understanding or invalidation of one's pain. As psychologist Carl Jung wrote, "Loneliness does not come from having no people about one, but from being unable to communicate the things that seem important to oneself." However, one can feel connected and supported when one does not have support systems at hand. There isn't a necessary number of supporters in this case, but rather a need for authentic connection, validation, care, and understanding.

When I had my near-death experience, I felt a sensation of intensified separation from everything and everyone around me. Those moments of suffocation put me in the greatest place of separation because, unlike the rest of the living world, my ability to breathe was taken from me. My consciousness was in a state of limbo when I could not use my body.

It was one of the scariest, loneliest places that I could imagine, even as a child. I had my family and friends rushing to my body, trying to save me and care for me. I saw them right in front of me, but no matter how hard I tried to express myself, they could not hear me. My body (or mortal instrument) was not working despite a deep yearning to be heard and listened to.

Within those brief moments in an intensified vista of darkness, I was filled with a fear of being stuck in such a state, deprived of my vital connection to others. That was when Spirit came through to me in the form of guides, angels, soul family members, and loved ones on the other side. A euphoric relief transpired. I felt a sense of joy, as well as a nearly comical reaction at the illusion of fear of losing my breath, life, and connection from others.

I was able to understand and remember what it was like to be a spirit on the other side, trying to communicate with loved ones on the earth plane. I learned that those on the other side are always there and want to communicate, but we can't always recognize their presence. In my experience, beings on the other side, particularly angels, are selfless and do not give up or get frustrated just because those on the earth plane do not or cannot listen.

What I learned next is how much more loved, supported, and protected we are than we realize. In those moments of intense suffocation, I found the greatest form of divine love always with me and beside me at every step and every breath and beyond. I will say I "re-remembered" this because during those moments I did not experience anything new. I just clearly connected to what was there on that side of the veil.

We truly have an entourage of support on the other side. In my case, there were two spirit guides I met, one male and one female. They seemed to lack any human experience in their energy and were a high octave of the spirit realm. They were and are the closest thing to my soul and had a transparent, selfless vision of caring.

I learned that those guides were there long before I descended into this lifetime, most importantly in the charting phase of what was important for this incarnation of my soul's journey of evolution. I also noticed that the presence of soul family members and angels surrounds us all the time. We will discuss the meaning and significance of our soul family and their significance soon. This taught me how closely we are being watched and loved by what I like to call the many satellites in heaven. They knew instantaneously what I was experiencing and hiding in my soul.

We tend to have an especially hard time here on earth when our true soul's nature has a memory of never needing to explain itself. After all, those around us watch and root for us with unconditional love for our development. This is something that not everyone experiences on the earth plane; in fact, those closest to us can hurt us the most by being cruel, not wanting the best for us, and not taking the time to love us unconditionally.

When the darkness inside my NDE turned to light, and when isolation was transformed to unfathomable understanding, care, and support, I could not believe how I forgot my spiritual nature and true home with its connection to family on the other side. It was through this that I was able to gain an awareness that this lifetime was not just a random biological coincidence with no purpose, meaning, or higher connection. Rather, this life is one of a spiritual purpose and profound connection.

I was not simply a flesh-and-blood human being. At my very core, who I was and what I was connected to was not from the earth but rather from the heavens. I recognized the divine spark that I was and the mystical, eternal being that I had been. We are all a part of what you can call God, higher consciousness, or source, and we are nothing less than pure love and perfection just as we are. To quote Ram Dass, "Our whole spiritual transformation brings us to the point where we realize that in our own being, we are enough."

Keeping this in mind, I recognized that embodying this realization was part of my duty within this lifetime. In my last incarnation, I got stuck and forgot the true essence of life. It was not the struggle of feeling stuck and trapped that led to me taking my life. In my limited awareness at that time, I was giving power to an illusion that I was not okay, I was not loved, and that in the end all would not be okay. In the midst of intense suffering, all I could see was pure darkness with no end out of my trap.

But this time, things would be different.

During my moments of suffocation, I caught a glimpse into the suffering of those who give up hope, but I also found reassurance that all is well. Light and love are always available. Light and love are all that ever was and is. When I assist those struggling with isolation and suffering in my personal practice, I am truly able to be with them and understand their feelings at the brink of wanting to throw it all away. I don't blame them. I realize how profoundly opposite their current feelings are with who they are at their core.

Another important concept I get to share is reminding others (and myself) about faith. Light is not something that waits at the end of a tunnel, and it's not a desperate hope for some miracle to occur to change one's perception. Rather, the miracle is recognizing that we are the very light of joy that we are seeking. We do not have to morph and evolve into something that we are chasing. Faith is about taking away all of the darkness and heaviness that covers our pure essence of joy, wisdom, grace, and connectivity.

Once I was able to see the Light, I recognized the illusion of suffering as something that exists as a dark illusion from all that is, which from my experience is pure Light. I recognized my drive to allow others to recognize they are much more loved, protected, and guided than they could ever imagine. Finding some ray of Light and giving power to it allows one to evolve and grow.

This can be a struggle for many of us because we live in a finite, linear world of limited awareness. It is hard to see past what we are going through right now, particularly when the present moment is filled with grief, pain, and suffering. In those circumstances, it's challenging to see a potential possibility of an alternate experience and the changes that would free us. I believe having others remind us of our guides, angels, and loved ones allows us to step past trying to do it all alone.

We should accept higher guidance and assistance from our entourage on the other side. Would you go to war as a one-man army or play basketball against a full team of opponents all by yourself? Yet in life we are taught that we have to muscle it all on our own, creating exhaustion, burnout, and hopelessness. As a psychotherapist, I have noticed that accepting help from others is seen as a sign of giving up in our culture. I have observed through my practice that those who accept that they need assistance are actually the strongest.

The most empowering act is when others evolve beyond cultural and family misconceptions and grow their perceptions of strength and grace. I often say that most of us were not born isolated in a cave. We are here with each other to learn not only how to coexist but to support, love, and nurture each other without living through destruction, isolation, and fear.

Having other subsequent out-of-body experiences later in life taught me correlations with isolation and suffering. When one feels isolated, there is a disconnection often leading to an addiction to negativity. A life experience becomes egocentric. Failing to remember that one is a spirit contributes to loneliness. Connectivity, expansion, and a care for others is nourishing to the soul. When one's ego is fed instead, it is a machine that is never properly satisfied, becoming an illusionary, seductive trap.

Hopefully, at some point in your life so far, you've given something to another person without expecting anything in return. Do you remember how that felt? No matter what the particular circumstances were, I've found that this is one of the greatest feelings. It reminds us that the fiber of our soul is connection and responsibility for each other. Generosity has the capacity to transcend our earthly plane because we are modeling ourselves after loved ones in the afterlife.

Through giving, one can recognize our undeniable connection to others and feel again an expanded sensation in the soul. Giving unconditionally heals the feelings of lifelessness and disconnection through seeing our capacity to ignite a fire of love and support in another. Gifts are constantly available in the heavens. Our decision here on earth is whether to open them up and believe we are worthy of them. Our license to do that at any time comes through our openness to receive and internalize.

Many people ask me what we do on the other side and what happens when it is our time to return home. From my experience, there are many levels on the other side when one passes. When I look back on soul family members, guides, angels, and understanding the eternal Light of God, the purpose of this lifetime was to embody those beings.

When I temporarily crossed over to the other side, the only thing that changed was perceiving the beauty of that realm and the feeling of heightened freedom and awareness. I was still myself and had my own personality but was surrounded by love.

I learned that it is hard to be on the other side and to rise up with other beings when we are not on the same level. For example, it is hard to feel like we can handle Harvard Law School without going through the previous grades and necessary steps. I learned that life itself is no different. We are here to learn how to implement all of the wisdom and awareness of real love, internalizing it just as beings from the other side provide it to us.

There are some barriers to this form of selfless love to oneself and another. From an early age, we are given the exact opposite experience of oneness: right away, we are separated by names, gender, age, race, physical bodies, and religions. These are all boxes that have the capacity to separate from others who do not fit into those particular, defined spaces.

But this lifetime is not so much about the earthly facts that we are taught. Instead, I invite you to try breaking down those boxes and putting into form the fundamental message that we are all connected to those in the heavens while on the earth plane. We are here to overcome the inherited illusions of separation from each other.

The pure essence of the other side is in caring for, giving to, and nurturing each being. On the other side, my soul did not transform into a celestial being. I was around celestial beings, but I took with me the observer that still could process life, have emotional reactions, and have a sense of development. That's when I was able to discover that my calling here was to allow others to remember their own eternity: we don't die. There is actually an infinite source of protection around all of us.

While there are many different unique paths, we are all learning how to bring in our true nature as loving, accepting, and nurturing beings within physical life. The soul has complete awareness, but at times here on earth that awareness is lost and forgotten. This impacts the soul's experience when it crosses over. Evolution of the soul enhances our experience of the earth plane but also allows us to evolve as higher spiritual beings when we cross over.

As Paramahansa Yogananda said, "To change, you have to make the effort. This world is the place to do it." We are to try to work on our own issues of anger, jealousy, competition, and selfishness. When we cross over, we can then more easily reawaken the divine and the gift that keeps on sourcing to contacted loved ones.

Remembering the simple truth that you are not alone can be helpful not only in times of loneliness but also in heightened times of emotional distress. As a child, I could not process or discuss my NDE with nearly anyone. Even though I felt more comfortable conversing with beings on the other side, I learned quickly that they could wait. I was meant to be here while staying connected.

I had to erase that sensation and connection to beings on the other side as a survival mechanism. When I was a teenager, I recognized that I was drowning in my own loneliness and needed that spiritual connection. In moments of intense trauma and distress, those beings would come to me and remind me that "we are here with you." In life's crossroads when I felt stuck, I allowed Spirit to take over and assist me in making decisions that were not from the limited vision of my mind but the unlimited vision of my soul.

In my near-death experience, I saw a sea of angels. Appearing as golden, childlike beings in front of me, they emanated the most gorgeous energies. They were looking down on me and the planet, sending healing. It was one of the most beautiful acts of grace and selflessness I had ever seen. Their extraordinary colors and sounds were incredibly striking. I saw beings that were there without agendas or judgments. They were here to just serve and provide warmth and comfort. I recognized at that moment that these angelic beings were here my entire life, in a dimension that was just a couple of clicks on the radio dial above.

I find that others feel alone for many reasons. Often, they feel that no one can join their feelings of freezing in darkness. I felt that same pain when I suffocated. I saw bodies around me, but they were breathing and trying to help me while I remained without a breath and totally disconnected from them. As a therapist and energy healer, I have tried my best to embody beings on the other side when others come to me. It does not mean that I do not get agitated at times or feel compassion fatigue. I am far from broadcasting that I am perfect. In my office, I surround myself with angels to remind me that they work through me with clients. They are a reminder to just be present, nonjudgmental, and accepting of others.

In my experience, these beings here with us not only help with our loneliness but they are part of the road to unconditional love and self-acceptance. Self-identity is usually not about formation but rather deconstruction. In our world and society, there is constant editing, checkboxes, and measuring of how we do against others. We are programmed from day one with the grades we receive in school. Later, we are conditioned to measure ourselves by how big our car or home is compared to our neighbors.

I've been able to remember, thanks to my NDE, that a big part of this lifetime is reminding ourselves of true self-love. Many of us were not born in awakened families or with school systems that would truly love us unconditionally. Rather, the expectation is that they will love us only if we fit their standards. In my experience on the other side, beings are there to remind us of who we truly are—loving, divine beings who are perfect just as we are. There is no one else like us. A profound teaching from Annie Kagan in her book *The Afterlife of Billy Fingers* is "if there is one thing worth living on the planet it is discovering self-love."

The act of self-love is a simple reminder to learn how to forgive and accept ourselves for all parts of who we are, what we like and what we don't. It does not mean that we have to love every action, for not every action is out of love. Some actions come out of an intense separation that has led to destruction of families, communities, and civilizations. The act of self-love is a selfless one that fills the void of emptiness, reminding ourselves that we are divine, perfect, and pure love. When we remind ourselves of our origin and the source of our lives, we begin to become a reflection of what it sees. I view self-love as being selfless because the more accepting we are of ourselves, the more tolerance, cohesion, mediation, and flexibility we can have with another. The way we perceive another, even our entire worldview, has a lot to do with how we perceive ourselves. At a higher level, the individual and collective are one and the same.

When I returned to my body, I struggled with the contrast of support, guidance, and pure love found on the other side compared to the harshness of the earth plane. Looking back, I recognize that I projected and judged my parents with the high standards of the unconditional love that I felt on the other side. Soon, we will discuss parental guides on the other side in the coming chapters. A lesson I learned is that my parents, as great as they were, are not God or beings on the other side. They, like everyone else, were learning in this earth school how to evolve and become more godlike through unconditional acceptance, care, and love for others.

I learned that not everyone was so connected, and furthermore not everyone was an earth angel. This lesson came through early on when I did not feel that same degree of attentiveness here that my parental guides provided on the other side. In this body, I just felt like an afterthought at home.

I developed a coping mechanism of retreating to the loving cocoon beyond this realm but recognized eventually that I had to find a way to do this human thing as much as I could. I had to learn to be comfortable in this world. Part of independence in our lives is a dependency on that Light to which we are always connected. This leaves us without an emotional and energetic need from others when they don't know how to treat us.

For the last couple of decades, I've learned the art of venturing out in the world and finding ways to remind myself of the separation from the Light and how to come back to it whenever I feel a lack of love or judgment from another. This has allowed me to live a life here on earth without a constant codependence on others or Spirit. A key has been learning to charge my batteries and reconnect to the source when needed.

The sensation of feeling down, isolated, and lonely goes against our fiber as true spiritual beings who are forever connected. Many forget this as they internalize the material externals on the outside. As we know, there are plenty of people who work tirelessly for all of the accessories of this world but have little time to use them with their family, making their pursuits empty.

I have found that many who struggle with loneliness forget not only what is around them and who they truly are, but also have internalized a checklist of their worthiness from others. Often, they have abandoned the notion that they are enough. I was once having a conversation with my friend Diane Richards, who is a professional medium and author of the book *Finding Emelyn*. During the conversation, spirit communication stepped through, and my grandfather came in. Because I look like a replica of him and we have similar personalities, this has not been the first time he has reached out to me from the other side.

"How can you be so hard on yourself?" my grandfather questioned through Diane. "To place doubt on yourself is to doubt me, and I am insulted by that because I am in you." I could tell from his tone that he was definitely in teacher-mode, not upset with me but trying to instill some confidence.

Many who feel alone have forgotten what they are connected to, much like I sometimes forget how connected I am to beings like my grandfather who continue to love me and teach me even after leaving this life. In this illusion, we can limit our unlimited power and sense of identity. I find that to accept yourself is to accept source, God, and Spirit. To reject yourself is the same, because we are in our essence Spirit and a ray of the divine.

I have developed a simple exercise every time I notice my energy or spirit dropping. It would be my honor to share it with you below in the hopes that it will also help remind you that you are never alone. You are connected, and you have the power to harness and strengthen that connection whenever you choose to do so. I use it simply to remind myself of my NDE, OBE, and other experiences.

I realize many others are disadvantaged if they didn't have angels and spirit guides put in their face like I did at such a young age. I do not find spiritual awareness to be associated with blind faith or putting power in fantasy. It is about evidential personal experience to shift belief into a clear knowing. At the basic level, improving the love that you have for yourself—taking it from conditional to unconditional—places you on the road map toward rising up and embodying your true nature as a loving, eternal, and mystical being.

Try this: think of the spirit realm as your own personal radio station. Our thoughts often cause disruption in the flow of frequency and connection to a station's clear message. Think of static radio sound as a way to understand how negative thinking affects connection to Spirit.

One of my favorite movies, *Hook* with Robin Williams, has a great allegorical reference for our true nature. Once Robin had a continuity of happy thoughts, he was able to fly and soar. I find it is the same way with our ability to connect and shift loneliness, sadness, and separation from Spirit into joy and euphoria.

Here is that brief, guided exercise that you can use to elevate your current state and learn how to tune into and sense Spirit. At the very least, it will improve your capacity to pivot and alter your feelings from lower consciousness to a higher one, with a heightened capacity to change your state of being.

Have a comfortable seat in your chair at home. You can also sit in your car or even lay in bed or on the floor.

Notice the flow of your breath. Allow yourself to take inventory of the miracles of those breaths. Recognize how millions of combinations of cellular communication and blood stream through you at one time. It is easy to get upset, but "gratitude will impact your altitude," as Zig Ziglar said.

Find something right now for which you are grateful. It could be a pet, family member, or obstacles you've overcome. Whatever comes to you, allow that thought to be allowed. Follow and embrace that feeling. If you don't think of anything or feel anything, at this moment focus on being grateful to breathe, to be safe, and to have an opportunity to be alive in this moment.

Let go of your prior worldviews and just be in this moment. Allow yourself to have a sensation of your favorite color flowing from the top of your head down to your feet. It might be violet, white, or gold—whatever comes to you. Even if you don't believe it, allow yourself to just see it. We are deciding to shift our power to beauty and grace and create a miracle with that shift of perception.

Feel this color surrounding you, protecting you, and guiding you. It cleanses darkness, pain, distress, and loneliness as you feel inseparable from this Light. You are the Light. If you desire to travel around the room, go back to a prior moment in life, or visit a loved one, smile through it and allow the warmth, love, and radiance of your color to fill you.

This is a time to recharge you and connect yourself back to the beauty that you always have been and are. If there is a loved one that you connect to, whether it be a guide, angel, family member, or pet, notice the reciprocal feeling of love and joy in reunification. Notice how pain, distress, and negativity can never separate you but rather only cause a temporary distraction for you and all of your loved ones watching you.

Take notice of how proud they are of you and your infinite strength, wisdom, and resiliency. Allow them to state their message and allow yourself to internalize the support, love, and guidance that they have for you. For you are forever connected to them, and they are forever connected to you.

As you become ready to open your eyes, notice a shift in how your body feels. You are now in a state of peace. You are a miracle to be alive, and you are capable of transforming a state of darkness, decay, and loneliness to Light. With a gentle touch, practice, and patience through this guided meditation, you too will be flying, evolving, and soaring toward all you have ever dreamed of.

Our lives are oftentimes built off our current sense of identity, attitude, and approaches to this existence. Our bricks are the foundation of our own home. Reminding ourselves that we are not separate from another becomes our calling to sustain the life that we are meant to live. It all begins with how we treat ourselves and begin to love ourselves.

The biggest source of separation is where we give our power. We sometimes give far too much weight to words spoken by someone who is jealous and angry, whose very goal was to bring us down. At times, I have done this, too, but I've found that I truly wished that other person understood how hurting another only hurts yourself.

Complicated transference of energy is often behind cruel words. Some are deeply rooted psychologically when a person takes out energy on a target that is safe rather than facing the actual source of conflict. As I said earlier, what we begin to feed tends to grow. When we consistently feed our true nature of a divine, loving being and remind ourselves of what we are connected to, we become capable of transforming ourselves and our perceptions of others when we get out of sorts.

This does not mean that we should not stand up to injustices. We need to speak up for those who do not have a voice. On a one-to-one basis, I remind myself that the person who is insulting me is in separation from me. I will give him compassion and understanding but never my self-approval. I will distance myself from that person while giving him or her love to return back to its source.

Now, remember one of the most important parts: the same applies to the self. As Marianne Williamson says in her book *Return to Love*, people can be mean, but we can be vicious toward ourselves. In my experience, finding ways to reconnect to angels and divine beings all around us places the eternal pedestal within this lifetime.

This is how it is supposed to be. Money itself is a currency that can heal and unify or divide and cause conflict depending on the source. We must understand the real source of a higher currency is unity, love, acceptance, and empathy. Through different practices of self-acceptance like journaling, pivoting negative self-talk, and the gentle reminder of listening to our unlimited currency and the forces around us, one can shift one's life to a pure connection to a source that keeps on giving.

Chapter Three: The Individual and The Collective

Children are living beings—more living than grown-up people who have built shells of habit around themselves. Therefore it is absolutely necessary for their mental health and development that they should not have mere schools for their lessons, but a world whose guiding spirit is personal love.

—Rabindranath Tagore

As a therapist who frequently deals with inter-family conflicts, I hear a particular phrase thrown around all the time: "You can't choose your family, so you have to put up with them or leave them." As a clinician, I choose to not get preachy in those moments and put my own spin on such a controversial topic, but instead I choose to observe that level of awareness and allow the individuals I am working with to process their own conclusions.

In breaking out of the chaos of my life, one of the most important outlooks was examining the perception of the root of chaos. If we see our lives as random, without order and purpose, then we see everything else that way too. With that mindset, challenges become burdens without a light at the end of suffering, or rather a light behind the darkness of suffering.

If there was one lesson within my NDE when it comes to conflict, it is that behind chaos there is a greater source of order. In fact, there is a masterpiece behind conflict. I do not believe that we came here to this planet to suffer but rather to thrive. This contrasts with the experience of many for whom life feels like a burden rather than a blessing in disguise.

When it comes to family, the order, opportunity, and method behind some of the madness is no different. Within my near-death experience and subsequent spiritual openings, I was made aware of two lessons:

1. This life in general and our family in particular are not random occurrences.
2. We come from our family, are connected to it but not created from or limited by it.

In my NDE, one of the most profound recollections I kept with me when I returned was how I was tied into what I refer to as soul family or tribe. When I crossed over, I became aware of family that I incarnated with throughout multiple lifetimes. Some took on roles as family members and others became my students when I worked as a teacher.

In my NDE and later throughout my life, I kept having dreams and visions of a large mountain cliff where I am surrounded by guides, angels, and my soul family. This setting and this scene that took place felt like I was getting ready to go off to a big mission here on the earth plane. In those memories, I recalled charting my life, including the people I would choose as my biological family, and other people and situations that I would encounter. It was as if higher guidance from the other side and I were collaboratively working on a game plan for a diet of the soul within this particular incarnation. Early on, I understood from those memories the illusion of seeing family or anything in our lives as random.

Looking at order through the lens of predictability is eye-opening too. When you think about it, out of the billions of people on the planet, the chances of you ending up where you are without some order is mind-blowing. Being with the family that you were born into, in a certain town, and with specific background circumstances has some profound significance. Those who struggle to find order and justice are not all tested the same in trials and tribulations, and not everyone has direct spiritual experiences to enhance clarity.

It is easy for my near-death experience to be perceived as a spiritual, cumulative, advantageous position for seeing the truth and light on the other side. I was also brought up in a family that provided me with a comfortable life that did not involve violence, drugs, or crime. It is difficult to accept this as it was challenging and at the same time rewarding. It certainly made life adjusting to the world and fitting in difficult but allowed for myself to learn to trust in a higher truth greater than the one I was experiencing.

I let go of attachment to the pain in this life many times and rose above it. I was able to do this by seeing this life as an experience but not a totality of existence. In other words, no matter what I went through, even facing death, there was a continuity and a travel of the soul beyond temporary experiences here on earth.

Each set of situations, no matter how difficult, are not a burden but an opportunity to rise above, grow, and blossom. It is hard to understand purpose when you feel burdened by an abusive parent or the opposite in having a child who is abusive to parents. Learning on a soul level means evolving information that aligns with our truths as well as shaping out of what does not align with us.

I look today at some of the biggest success stories or most loving parents and I find that they did not come to those places by happenstance. The common denominators of disappointment, failure, and mistreatment from others acted as fuel for their fire to be better than the patterns and circumstances they were handed.

Finding the higher divine order in perception of all of life can lead to wisdom, grace, and ease in navigating otherwise challenging and cumbersome situations. This was one of the keys and allegorical references of my NDE. It taught me that heaven, the other side, and Light were not some far-out place or in some religiously pious individual's hands. They were the essence of who I truly was and where I came from.

This knowledge allowed me to entrust that I was forever connected to the heavens and my soul family in those moments when I did not feel supported, validated, or understood. If you experience an especially difficult family background, I feel there will be great healing when you tap into that deep, eternal place that exists for each and every one of us.

By doing so, navigating those moments of disconnection from your true fabric of unconditional love and support and finding independence from others will happen more easily. We'll cover exactly how you can also master this in subsequent chapters.

I learned about the role of past lives in my near-death experience and how they can blur lines within family and interpersonal relationships. Without recognizing it at times, people find a particular degree of adjustment to parents, children, and others in their family roles. Sometimes a power struggle happens when one sibling tries to parent another or a child tries to parent a parent.

Being informed of the bigger picture of the deeper reasons for role uncertainty is helpful. In my case, my challenging and competitive drive in many ways came from a lack of acceptance and awareness of my father in his paternal role. I was an older brother to him in another lifetime. Having an acceptance of the changing of tides and reasons behind the competition allowed me to embrace my father for his role while being aware on a deeper level of the times that I push my subconscious Achilles' heel.

I learned in my NDE that the soul is here to evolve karmically. I also believe that the soul is not a discrete entity but rather an element of the greater collective whole. I look at family not as a biological random occurrence that could feel like a burden and source of anger at God and the universe. Instead, I invite you to embrace the idea that family is a collective team that is here to teach each other. We often forget that this lifetime is in a way a play where each member fulfills a different role to help evolve the rest. Some of these roles can lead to indirect or direct opportunities of growth and evolution. Free will and choice are at the core of this experience for us.

For skeptics out there who are rolling their eyes at this talk from someone of a relatively privileged background, I understand the frustration. At times family can be anything but what it should be: supportive. What should you do with family members who are abusive and cruel? Should you continue to embrace them and try to work things out?

I would answer that each person has a different role and dynamic within an individual soul's journey. At times learning to be empowered against another who is abusive can be a soul lesson or karmic tie for that soul who needs to integrate personal empowerment and courage to stand up to others. Love is not always singing "Kumbaya" around the fire. Sometimes you have to love yourself more than another and leave a situation.

I would say to go with what feels right within your core. When we start to look at family and at life, take the time to consider that there is a greater reason for any issues. Then, our actions and approaches can lead to more patience, diplomacy, and mediation within a big-picture perspective rather than the simmering annoyance of conflict that meets the eye.

Merely looking at life with the lens that it has a purpose can add up some of the pieces of our own purpose, which includes family. Even if you don't believe in a divine order, the basic approach is looking at life as a play and a game to test your inner strength.

When a family member is cruel to you, you can say, "She is a good actress and it is my choice to give her the power of my anger or to step back from my emotion, observe what is happening, and own my reaction as merely a response to an unmet need within myself." Through my NDE, I learned not only the pattern of karma and soul growth but also the interconnected elements. Another's action is not just a mirror of what is inside. That soul is a direct mirror to my soul because all souls are connected in some way.

My family members are the first when I act out to tell me to read my own book. I appreciate this about my family. While family can be extremely rewarding, given the intense karmic ties plus the time spent within this lifetime, our family members can truly know how to push our buttons.

As Ram Dass said, "If you think you are enlightened go and spend a week with your family." They do not see the good front that we try to put in front of others in our professional roles and dynamics. They have seen us at our worst, and that image is a part of them. There is a comfort level where family members are not afraid to mess up and get angry because no one is worried about losing a job. Having said that, when I look back, the times that I was best able to handle conflict with family members was when I considered the situation from a broader perspective.

One example of this illustration came from a profound, transformative experience mentioned in my last book. I was asked to leave my home temporarily due to acting out. Looking back, I can fully understand my parents' reasoning. But I felt like the plug of life was taken from me. I decided to walk to a local playground. While there, I was reminded of the playground where I had my near-death experience.

Home was not something limited and created from biology but experienced through it. I could have felt displaced but instead it was a reminder of the impermanence of all and the greater belonging to a home. This allowed me to feel comfort and the awareness that others play roles as teachers in life. Oftentimes, these are difficult lessons on the surface but teach us to strengthen ourselves and see past the lens that we are looking through. I knew that I was a child forever home in God's playground, and this experience here on earth was just an experience but not my ultimate residence of dwelling.

One thing that doesn't pass easily is the ability to mend fences and find new ways to love. Sometimes, it's more important to work things out than be right. Ideally, finding ways to rectify conflicts and focus on the eternity that comes out of love rather than the short ego high from being right in a dynamic should motivate mediation of conflicts.

I had to learn to improve on this. Certainly, I was no picnic as a child and was a great disrupter. Reminding myself of the wisdom gained in my NDE about the elements of soul family and importance of working things out, mediation is as helpful to elevate the team's state as well as your own. Heaven is not far away and separate from this life but a continuum of what you took with you in your lifetime—your lessons and your growth.

Family is one of the most important lessons that we have. The greatest lesson that I learned regarding family is to be cognizant of the contract that tied you and that family member together. This is a gentle reminder that there is a spiritual lesson beyond what we're going through now. The charting plan by God, Spirit, or whatever source you label was a part of that. The darkness and light that we find in family applies through life. Keeping this in mind can help the testiness of the dark by remembering the eternal Light behind and together within each family member.

The classroom mentality is helpful to improve my ability to manage conflict. When I sense agitation and the frustration of disappointing myself or others, I find much wisdom in the Buddhist principle that that person is teaching me something. As Buddhist teacher Pema Chödrön said, "Nothing ever goes away until it has taught us what we need to know." Mindfulness has been one of the key elements to help me out in life. I have learned through mindfulness to take away judgment of another and to be the observer in life and what is happening.

Within my near-death experience, I understood that the soul can be described as a constant, silent voice of observation within. The family that we are born into can influence us at multiple levels with ideologies, belief systems, and attitudes. I find that going within through meditation or being keenly aware of how we are processing what is happening to us and not just reacting to it leads to empowerment, wisdom, and the skill to choose how we will handle others.

With practice, this can lead to more ingrained repetition of taking the high road with those in our family. A mindful approach is key to healthy family dynamics or any other relationship. It creates freedom not with what another did to us but how we choose to handle, respond, and perceive it. Family and their presence in our lives can be seen the same way as a whole. Considering them to be a gift to our souls, a lesson, or a teacher—whichever fits the particular dynamic—assists in seeing past the surface.

As a professional Past Life Regression Practitioner, I can attest firsthand to the value of Past Life Regression in the areas of unexplained trauma, life's purpose, and interpersonal relationships, including with family members. Past Life Regression is a form of hypnosis that helps clients to access what I call the database, or what some call the higher mind.

Often referred to as the subconscious, the higher mind has a wealth of information from this lifetime. It is believed that the subconscious mind also has access to intelligence and awareness of our past lives. Often, clients who come to my seminars or private sessions explain that they have tried to see therapists for family therapy or individual therapy, but they still can't understand why their parents were or are so cruel to them or why their spouse treats them like a child.

Clinical psychiatrist Dr. Brian L. Weiss, a pioneer of Past Life Regression, wrote that "without understanding, patterns tend to repeat, unnecessarily damaging the relationship." Often within multiple sessions, layers of repetitive tendencies from others are uncovered and explained. This helps clients become conscious of the unconscious tendencies and repetitive behaviors carried over from others in their lives.

This leads to putting some of the pieces of the puzzle together and helps clients move forward with grace, ease, and wisdom through deeper understanding of the roots beneath the branches. This leads to beginning to see the divine hand of a higher source in their life through an evolved awareness. As the messages from the sessions are integrated, clients find that those painful lessons in the school of life no longer need to be embraced.

Growing up after my near-death experience at such a young age was hard. I was trying to fit in and please my parents, but I was ignoring something inside of me. It felt like what I saw on the other side was a secret that I needed to keep private, push away, and hide. That knowledge was like a beach ball that I kept on trying to push down to the bottom of the water, but it kept creeping up to the surface through indirect recollections or other spontaneous mystical experiences and insights.

For all the parents reading this, I know I am not alone. In fact, I am sure there are plenty of children out there today who, like myself, have had near-death experiences, psychic phenomena, or other mystical experiences. I say this with respect because I find children to be one of the most misunderstood age demographics on the planet. The level of insight and maturation associated with the physical body and its age is often the source of its problem.

Once we see all family members, including children, for their core, things begin to start to shift. What I learned from my perspective is that I needed to integrate the wisdom from my near-death experience in my lifetime. The big-picture goal was to help others. One of those lessons was the lack of randomness, the synchronicity, and the divine hand behind all of life's interactions when seen through the eyes of the sacred observer or the soul.

Family was one of the most challenging elements from my perspective. As great as my parents and the life I was expected to live were, they were in stark contrast to what I experienced on the other side before I came to this planet. For other children, it is no different. I believe that an infant's crying is not just for biological-based reasons such as teeth growing in. There is a big adjustment phase for children when they come to earth as they integrate from the unconditional love and existence as a euphoric, mystical being on the other side.

It would be helpful for parents if society altered its perception toward children. Regarding a child with appreciation for his or her unique wisdom gained through so many lifetimes and the higher power and plan that connected that child to a parent and family helps caregivers understand them at a profound level. While they show us a playful, simple, and joy-filled side of this life, kids are dealing with a lot of adjustments to their bodies, their worlds, new families, and new roles they accepted as a soul.

Although it takes time to form words and develop an outer self-expression, on a soul level they know what is happening and are taking it all in. Having my near-death experience put me in a foreign world of isolation. I struggled to comprehend and then accept that others did not see what I saw in my experience. They had forgotten their connection to the other side. Having a degree of understanding of what kids are truly going through is imperative. Awareness of a child's intelligence should shift to include the soul and its conflicts and needs. Consider that, in each child, you are not looking at a body but a pure divine being just as yourself.

It is important to find ways to operate not from judgment or an emotional standpoint but from a soul level. If you can take a step back and speak to your child as a grown person (a.k.a., the grown soul that they actually are inside), and do so with empathy, concern, and validation for their current defiance, it makes a world of a difference. They are, after all, an evolved spiritual being far greater than the presented child in front of you.

Education and religion were two of the most difficult adjustments for me to make on this planet. I struggled to accept them for the majority of my life. Parents often focus too much on what academic track their kid is on and what they will turn into, whether he or she will become a doctor, a lawyer, or an engineer. They do not consider who their child is as a soul.

When an individual who is overtly experiencing trauma, anxiety, or depression comes to our doors, we would be more likely to understand and have more compassion than we do for children who we force to fit a mold. If we are to believe that each child is unique, it is important to treat a child accordingly rather than as a projected image of what is important to a parent and family background.

It is probably no surprise that elements of religion were tough for me as a child. I was taught a description of a jealous, conditional, chauvinistic, and abusive God, which did not fit with what I experienced with my soul. I find that religion is an important part of raising a child as it provides structure. A more important element, however, is encouraging a child to be able to understand his or her own spiritual awareness and to be empowered and not disempowered through fear gained in religion.

It is counter to many religions to go within for answers because there is an obligation to go by the book. It is important to see children as spiritual beings with their own unique wisdom to be listened to. I disagree with the outlook of seeing children as blank canvases. This is the furthest from truth as children are fully aware of their multidimensional being and intelligence, maybe more so than adults who become trapped within their earthly conditioning.

Finding ways to listen more to children instead of trying to color in an inherited belief system will empower them with who they are and their unique personality and purpose. Then they will not merely be trained to act on what they have been taught, which is a regurgitation from family members.

I also struggled with the difficult misalignment of what I was connected to in spirit. Through my NDE, my form of spirituality came in the source of angels, an encounter with an awareness of Christ, soul family members, and spiritual guides. This was my form of belief and worldview. I have found angels and past life awareness spread throughout religions, but it was not exactly the focal point of my religious education.

It is said that Jesus himself spoke of past lives, and this was later banned by Constantine at the Council of Nicaea due largely to fear and control. The same tendency applies in raising children. Adults have a subconscious or conscious fear of how truly powerful and aware children are, which brings a desire to prevent them from potentially disrupting tradition.

It is important for parents to be sensitive to the fact that kids may be in another place in their minds and hearts. Therefore, we should not enforce conformity but allow children to express what they are seeing, feeling, and knowing without passing judgment. As a therapist, I've found that clients who might have had mystical experiences are bogged down by the level of judgment and ridicule from those surrounding them. This is nothing new.

It has happened to so many with a groundbreaking idea, whether it be Sigmund Freud early on in his career, religious figures such as Buddha by his family members, Joseph from the Old Testament by his siblings, and Christ by government officials and others. As Wayne Dyer said, "When you judge another, you do not define them, you define yourself."

It is important to never set limits on what a child is connected to because they have a closer and more sensitized connection to the spirit world than others. The key is for the child to live that out so that his or her life is more easily navigated through the grace of Spirit.

Reminding ourselves that we are souls no different from our children and that we were once in their position will help create a system that does not try to box in the child. We will not attempt to control their lives but guide them gently into learning more about who they are and their unique individual needs.

Redefining children as beings who have infinite wisdom to cultivate is crucial. As their assignment from the other side, this wisdom is meant to be remembered and developed. It is the most important responsibility of their human life and the main goal of their life's education. When a family encourages and supports a child, that child will have the ability to amaze their parents with inherently unlimited clarity.

There are countless stories of children remembering their own past lives, including past traumas. At an early age, Buddhist monks and lamas are tested based on their degree of recollection from their last lifetime. This is critical if they are to take their own past life successor's position. I find that it is important for kids to process their own past lives with the ability to understand that this life is a new page and chapter. They are to draw wisdom and lessons from the past and integrate them in the present.

Understanding the self translates to how we perceive another within our family. The chain of family members in our lives is eternal, much like ourselves. Within my near-death experience, I had an awareness that soul family extends beyond individuals in biological links. I believe that the earth and all its inhabitants are truly soul family at the end of the day. I use the term "soul family" to refer to the innermost circle and tribe that have incarnated countless times as lessons are learned and collective evolution takes place.

Much like the earth itself, everything changes when you see it as a reflection of yourself rather than something to manipulate for your own needs. The important element is to overcome the rush of materialistic greed for the self and to regard and care for others as a part of this one family. Once we start to see life through a soulful lens, whether that be in looking at a child, family member, or difficult coworker, everything changes.

We are reminded even in the worst times that while the actions of a person may divert from that of a loving family member when spiritual awareness is dimmed, at the deepest core, all that remains is pure consciousness and awareness as one tribe. After my NDE, I was moved to remind others of their true home and that this life is as a fleeting dream.

Through overcoming illusions of separateness with divine grace, the veil to the other side becomes thinner and less distant. Heaven can wait when we cultivate it with our human family. As Wayne Dyer wrote, "Heaven on Earth is a choice you must make, not a place you must find." That understanding of eternity has helped me to comprehend love as the ultimate measurement of a life. With a reminder of heaven as the ultimate unifier—the soul's origin and eternal home for each of us—we will naturally reject all that does not strive to align with this awareness.

Chapter Four: The Light at the End of the Ladder

There is a light within each of us that can never be diminished or extinguished. It can only be obscured by forgetting who we are.
—Deepak Chopra

During a particular part of my NDE, I became aware that a ladder in this world is much different from a ladder in the other world. In the Western world where I was raised, a ladder is often symbolic of material success. We go from one car to a nicer car, a house to a more expensive house, and a job to the next better position as we climb the rungs of life's ladder. We are often taught that to be happy we need to get that next upgrade. Even phone companies will slow down data usage for us to get a new upgrade. Everything is about minute-to-minute advancement in keeping up with the Joneses.

But where is this next rung really leading to? What is the sum total of the material rungs that so many are climbing, sweating, and putting every life-force into? Can we take the house, car, job, or life earnings with us when we leave this world? I often contemplate this ladder that was taught to me. The material success found at the top of that ladder is all that matters.

There are two phrases from famous Swiss psychiatrist and renowned psychoanalyst Carl Jung that I love. In his reference to the stages of life, he said, "Thoroughly unprepared, we take the step into the afternoon of life. Worse still, we take this step with the false presupposition that our truths and our ideals will serve us as hitherto. But we cannot live the afternoon of life according to the program of life's morning, for what was great in the morning will be little at evening and what in the morning was true, at evening will have become a lie."

The *morning* of life is represented by the ego-driven hustle to climb the ladder of success as a benchmark for self-identity. The *afternoon* of life is about identifying what you can't take with you and how you can find beauty and meaning in life. Many people throughout life fluctuate between stages, and some—up until their last days—are focused on the morning of life.

Yet, in most cases, when someone is about to knowingly leave their body, they focus on the most meaningful stage, which is the energy of love. The love that we have given and received is all that matters when we leave our human bodies. I used to struggle with measuring up to the standards of the world and its values as synonymous with my self-identify versus what is truly important: the evening stage of life.

The truth that I experienced in my NDE was that I was not judged for what I did but rather I was loved for who I was. And I knew I was to learn how to be authentically "me." So many people struggle with their self-identity as if it is directly tied to the rungs on the ladder. I think part of the struggle is that the current status or rung in the ladder that you are on has no true basis for what is important beyond your human life.

Think of the body that you are: many identify as their human self, but your physical body is not something that you can take with you when you die. There is so much instability in the world around me. It all comes back to foundation. As I reference Jesus time and again, one who has a solid foundation will not be swayed by the winds, or a tree that is deeply planted and rooted will withstand the strong winds of life. Material objects are not the foundation of life.

Climbing the rungs on the ladder of life is not the goal of our human experience. The foundation of life, and what is eternally important, is immaterial. Love is what matters. You are not the sum of acquired wealth and status, but instead your value is how you give and receive love. It is no wonder why so many people are stressed, as they are living their life for temporary meaning instead of living for eternity.

During his seminars, Wayne Dyer often asked his participants, "If you could squeeze an orange out what would come out?"

Many would raise their hands and just state simply, "Orange juice." He would then add that if you were to squeeze yourself out, what would be left? I am sure the majority of us might have to think about this. What truly would be left if you took everything away and got down to our basic essence? All of our superficial identities and egos would fade away. And all that would remain is the love that you are and the love that you shared. Love truly overcomes any form of death.

The ladder is a major theme when it comes to growth, expansion, and meaning. It is significant to have a perspective and point on the ladder that shows growth that you had and where you are headed. The ladder is not for material success but rather a ladder to return back to your own source as a divine masterpiece.

I love how my good friend and author of *The Mindful Athlete* George Mumford often says, "If you do not know who you are you can be anybody, and if you do not know where you are going you can be anywhere." I simply think it's important to take note of the GPS and of the direction of our soul in its relationship to higher awareness. Stop and reflect: Who am I? What am I doing in this world? What am I living for? What is truly important?

Our perspective reflects what we are living for. If our goals are finite, then our motives will be driven by limited motives and energies. If our perspective is one of eternal significance, then we live out our human experience with the goal of loving ourselves and everyone else.

At the top of the *true* ladder is an eternal Light. It is our ultimate goal to find ways to transcend the ladder of the *morning* of life with its finite nature of satisfaction of the ego and live our lives in the infinite realm. Eckhart Tolle, the best-selling author of *The Power of Now,* said it best: "Death is a stripping away of all that is not you. The secret of life is to 'die before you die'... And find that there is no death."

I believe before we entered this life, or what some refer to as the "charting phase" of life, there were preset criteria and different rungs on the ladder that we were to go through. Some view the different steps of the ladder as a burden or a school. I often look back at these steps as finding ways and opportunities to spiritually evolve and grow.

Having a growth mindset in life on each step of the ladder is a mindset that can influence your life. Our overall energy and drive behind our growth is important. We can live our lives for what truly lasts, meaning something that we can take with us when we leave. Rumi the Sufi poet stated, "From the moment you came into this world, a ladder was placed in front of you that you might transcend it."

We are often taught that when we do right or a good thing we get a reward, and when we do a bad thing, we are punished. I find that this often creates a life based on fear of being eternally condemned for our choices and actions. One typically does not act out of love or the embodiment of love as much as they act out of fear.

Have you ever found that when you truly love something you want to just share it with the world? Love is like this and has a lasting impact on change. Fear, negativity, and judgment cannot last in the true waters of love. When we are in those waters, we want others to join us and to be there with us.

Once I let go of the ladder out of fear of suffocation and eternal suffering, I was able to access the eternal Light of Spirit. So much of what I experienced was not based off Spirit but based off what I was taught. The fear in the moment was only the value that I gave it. Once I let go of that fear, I inhaled an eternal breath of loving awareness of the other side that could never be taken away. It is the ultimate reality. I let go of the temporary ladder that I was standing on and entered the eternal Light.

Our steps, rhythms, and energy are everything. When dancing in this life and climbing the ladder, we can remind ourselves that we are eternal, spiritual beings here on earth having this human experience. I am to remember who I truly am on each step. Sometimes in life we have the foundation of the ladder rungs pulled and feel as if we have lost our footing or fallen. It is important to understand that as above, so below. The eternal Light on top of the ladder is also in each step and will catch us even if we "fall." Our foundations being pulled is our spiritual growth and it is actually a blessing.

So often we think we are in control of outer circumstances and can feel victimized by them. We can become, at times, cynical and angry at God for having rungs pulled out from under us on the ladder of life. Reminding ourselves that there is a far greater intelligence than our own awareness at play and trusting in the light and peace over everything else is a key to living a life for eternity.

No matter what we are going through, we have to remind ourselves that our perception of the event will alter the actual event. Choose a perspective viewing everything from a lens of love. In my NDE, I could have chosen to be in a state of fear, disbelief, and disharmony with my true nature. The moment I chose love was when I was given my life back. I recognized that I had really died at the age of three long before those moments on the ladder in the park. Once I remembered this, I remembered all that was real, lasting, and truly mattered. So many times in life people will say and think "when this set of criteria works out, I will then be peaceful and happy."

I think it is important to understand our superpower lies in understanding our engagement with stimuli-influenced perception. The moment we choose something is the moment we feel it. Once you decide to have a peaceful journey on the ladder of life, embracing opportunities of evolution and bringing heaven to each life event, you are given an opportunity to fill that space with peace. It is therefore not when things happen as I would like them to happen, when I choose peace, joy, and so on, but rather once I choose peace and joy is when these things are experienced.

The egoic ladder is often like chasing a never-ending carrot on a stick; each step that we take gives us a temporary high, but nothing lasting. Once we lose what we were trying to gain, or fail at our pursuit, the temporary high is gone, and we are left looking for the next rung to climb. I always try to remember on each step of the ladder to look for the light. When our energy is uplifted, we are in Spirit. Finding different ways to be that spiritual being on the steps of the ladder is how we can truly be on a guided path.

As I reflect on all of the great spiritual teachers and their ascensions, it was never an easy path. Some of their paths, like Buddha, required them to leave the ladder that their family wanted them to climb (like a specific area of study or career choice). The foundation of spiritual teachers and masters was not created to be a pedestal on the ladder, but a great reminder of the individual potential bestowed in each one of us.

I fully embrace the notion that each step of the ladder was designed as not something that we cannot do or handle but something that we can eventually embrace and work with. We can find ways to not rely on our own energy to climb each rung, but we can learn to integrate the endless light of the top of the ladder. This will allow us to experience a sense of "light on the journey." We are here to remind ourselves of the eternal Light within and to shine to others. When you see another who might struggle and resist the step they're currently on, send them good thoughts and energy for their evolution and the ability to let go of their resistance. What we resist persists; what we let go allows life to grow.

I learned from my NDE that I did not need to take a spaceship to go to the other side or to ace every rung on the ladder to go to heaven. I truly understood that I was not only here as a spiritual being to create heaven on earth, but that I have always been and will always be a part of heaven on earth. I did not need to rise to the top to get to heaven; rather, heaven was always in my own backyard.

I use "the other side" as it is a conventional term that many understand, but I prefer to call it "home." You don't need to get a ladder to get to home, as home is who you are. You can continue to express your true self and become a grander expression of the source within. I learned that each lifetime with its many different experiences, themes, roles, lessons, or karma—a Hinduism principle for the sum total of one's action of dharma, or one's duty or role in life—can be a different rung of a ladder.

With each rung we are getting away from what Edgar Cayce describes as "involution," or the process of getting away from God, which can occur within lifetimes to finding ways to become closer to God. The idea is that we don't need to go on a ladder within lifetimes. We can embody who we are at the top and don't need rungs to separate ourselves or have a route to our destination but embody the destination itself with no separation.

It is my hope that we do not have to wait until we die to feel full of life, but rather to live each step while we are alive. Being truly alive is awakening from the dream of being separate from the light on the other side and connecting to it in all that we do.

As souls, much like the angels on Jacob's ladder, we love the concept of going up and down in life through a series of involution and feel distance or forgetfulness in our awareness, apart from God. Our world falls in love with these kinds of stories of those who fall and come back (the prodigal son). The truth is, we can never be truly ever separated from God, as love and eternity cannot be cut up or divided. There is no separation (Romans 8:32). What is limited in the awareness of the mind never leaves the eternal unlimited awareness of our nature.

The idea is to not return home when our bodies are buried, but to take home/love with us on our journey in the human body. We think that we are stuck here or are separate, but we are truly always home. We can, through loving awareness of God, be in this earth but not of this earth and forever connected to home while in the body. We don't need anything or to change anything that limits the mind when it is actualized in the soul while we are having a human experience. This is being an angel in human form or an enlightened aware (spiritual) being.

Chapter Five: Transforming Grief to a Knowing

And those who were seen dancing were thought to be insane by those who could not hear the music.
—Friedrich Nietzsche

Throughout life, I have looked at death through many different eyes and lenses. As a child, when others were upset about a loved one passing away, I wrestled with the term "death" and did not know quite what to make of it.

When I saw others grieving losses in the years after I returned from my NDE, I recognized that the biggest and unrecognized death for many was the loss of awareness and the blindness that came from forgetting their eternity. I saw how many held the illusion that they could ever die.

As I got older, I understood the reasons for tears. In a material world where many are completely identified with their bodies, I could see how the greatest of fears would arise when a loved one transitioned. It seemed like all of the good times, memories, and joy were replaced by a six-foot pit, a hole of pure darkness. The prospect of this happening to someone close to you and at an unknown point in the future can be terrifying.

Many of us have experienced this, causing great distress, panic, and anxiety. Some families in our society will do all they can to hold on to a family member, channeling their need for comfort into pushing away the inevitable. This sometimes sidesteps recognition of the suffering that a loved one is enduring rather than honoring them and learning to accept the flow of the tides of the seasons of life.

Hearing news of a loss can be a sudden shock and trauma to one's system. Some losses can be accepted with grace or letting go. I believe grief and the varied perspectives of a loss of a loved one is rooted in both biology and in cultural upbringing. Animals grieve loved ones, showing it is seemingly natural to become emotional over endings of the light that the individual was and the darkness and emptiness that now is left without their presence.

Forms of grief are influenced by foundational beliefs gained through cultural, religious, and family outlooks. Some cultures in Africa and Central America and Ireland for example choose to celebrate the loss of a loved one through dance, drink, good food, and stories. These examples are traditions of grieving loved ones through choosing to celebrate their continuity.

I believe that everyone has their own unique style of grief. Foundationally as a therapist, I have been influenced by the late Dr. Elisabeth Kübler-Ross, well-known Swiss American psychiatrist and pioneer of the hospice movement. In her book *Death and Dying,* Dr. Kübler-Ross speaks of the five stages of grief as denial, anger, bargaining, depression, and the final stage of acceptance.

Acceptance, based on her work, does not imply that one sees agreement or justification of the fairness in our loss but rather an acknowledgment of our ability to move forward. I have come to learn that grief and its stages aren't limited to the loss of a loved one. The process is an umbrella for an entire range of life circumstances that go through their own cycle of ending.

Death has been misused and poorly represented when it comes to the loss of a loved one. I agree with the great Dr. Raymond Moody when he chose to write his pioneering *Life After Life.* His case studies showcase those who have had near-death experiences to inform about what awaits us on the other side of the veil. In this book, Dr. Moody even officially coined the term near-death experience.

It was a groundbreaking publication in the mid-1970s and looked at life after death through a philosophical and scientific lens. The terminology of "life after life" instead of merely "death" is quite fitting and helpful. The words that we choose in this life can shape perceptions of death.

When we say the word "death," notice what happens to us through a purely physiological basis because of how we are wired. We nearly can become the connotations of the word and begin to shut down to a dark place. "Life" is just the opposite, opening new doors of infinite possibilities.

I learned on a personal and experiential level that "death" is the furthest word to describe what happens when the physical body dies. On the other side was a pure sensation of euphoria, clarity, and the truth and familiarity of being fully alive. Looking at my own human lifetime, I have had glimpses and tastes of these sensations. In contrast, the full light of eternity was blasted on me in every possible way when I had my near-death experience.

Many may ask, what can the dead or dying teach the living? I am not dead, but I have been nearly dead, and my experience taught me a few different points. The first basic lesson is this: we don't die! I have learned that, yes, there is a dying and even a grieving phase for what was. When I was on the other side and contemplating the choice to live or die, part of my soul was in grief over losing what I had, but more importantly, it was grieving what I could be.

In the spirit realm, those fears were dispensed by my awareness of time. I understood that all the parts of us are not trapped in one dimension of time. The truth is quite the opposite: we are unlimited in who, what, and where we are. Essentially, the past, present, and future create an endless story of endless possibilities. I learned that our choices to take a particular angle toward this endless matrix of possibilities can influence but not dictate who we are. Our lives are much like a river that constantly flows and is forever changing its boundaries and path. So, too, is our soul's path as we evolve throughout different lifetimes.

Life after death is not just possible when a loved one dies. It's also possible for surviving loved ones. With my clients, I have worked on looking at grief through a sense of belief. A man named James was grieving a loved one. It was recommended that James go through his reactions on an emotional, psychological level. I instructed James to not resist grief but to simply allow it to pass and experience it.

On the other side of grief, James found a transformed belief. In a sense, by not resisting he was able to work toward the higher awareness aspects of grief. Through this, he was able to understand that the loved one that he was grieving was forever connected to him but did not belong to him.

James recognized that the soul had a journey beyond this body, just as he did. The body did not create the love but rather was a tool and experience for the particular soul. Through this awareness, James found it possible to not only believe in life after death of a loved one, but to find life after death in his own life. James was able to understand that the soul did not mourn the transformation. Both James and his loved one could move beyond the notion that there can only be this life.

Death is a human construct and experience, and it speaks antithetical to the experience of the soul. The story of the soul is eternal and timeless. The story of the human experience is time bound and linear. It is important to not bypass this but to pass through this part of ourselves that processes life through this awareness.

We should be informed of the human aspect of consciousness but not enslaved by it. I mean we do not want to bury and suppress our grief but rather honor it. In the backs of our minds, we can hold a greater wisdom and truth of eternity for that loved one. The emotional human part of us can accept this loss, but something deep in us yearns and has a greater knowing that there was never a loss in the first place.

That love truly never ends. The bonds between us are not only possible but even stronger through death. There have been moments in my life where I was close to a loved one who was struggling at the end. Through their passing, I was able to find a stronger connection than before. They didn't put me on hold or had activities to do or life getting in the way; now, I am able to have full connection and contact with the crossed-over loved one.

I learned that death overcomes the human illusion of fame as well. In my life, I have connected with many celebrities and have identified with them. I have gotten names that no one knows that I connect to on a regular basis that put me in a deep place. During a recent mediumship reading that I had with a stellar local medium named Tony Russo, she paused and started singing a few lyrics from "Islands in the Stream."

She paused and met my eyes. "Jake," Tony began, "Kenny Rogers is here. He is telling me that he likes your teachings and what you do. He guides you."

I sat there, speechless. My human side questioned, who am I for Kenny Rogers to give attention to? But another aspect of me had a knowing that there is no true VIP or barrier to souls, however ascended they are in their life that their consciousness is accessible and connected to all. There are high energies on the other side as well, and many are able to have an even stronger connection and certainly have an easier time reaching them or being noticed than in this life.

I learned from being near death that my soul can never be terminated. In those moments of suffocation, I was able to understand myself not as a physical being but rather as an endless, energetic spiritual being. It was clearly and keenly known in those moments that the fear that many have of dying and experiencing pure darkness and emptiness could not be further from the truth. I learned, much like Ram Dass would say, that the true essence of my soul was eternal "loving awareness" that could never be broken.

Throughout their lifetimes, many choose to identify themselves with body and ego, not the soul, and thus fall into a trap of the linear, the finite, and their limitations. Another lesson I understood is that love between those in the heavens and those here on earth is eternal. It was evident through the greetings of soul family members, spiritual guides, and angels within the heavens that all is connected. I learned that life here on earth is just as connected to that side. They are always here for us unconditionally, watching us and giving us nudges.

When I came back, I felt a sense of comedy when seeing others distressed and concerned. I learned that we don't have to worry when losing loved ones. They are fine. What is important for us to learn from their position is how to be free, much like they are. Honor those who have gone to the heavens, or from what I experienced, those who are experiencing a rebirth period through the freedom they gained.

I have found in both my personal and professional lives that grief for losing a loved one is much like the trajectory of eternity that their loved ones experience—nonlinear. It does not have a timetable or expiration date. At times after losing a loved one, we can be totally fine for weeks on end, but then a raw pain tsunami of emotion can hit us out of nowhere. Grief for a loved one can certainly be like the ocean. At times, the water is at a high intensity, and at other times there is calm at sea. Grief runs its natural course. The important part is to let nature flow and unfold just as it should.

For me, knowing the eternity of the soul as a child led to a difficult time understanding funerals, death, and dying. My understanding even caused me to laugh at the seeming comedy of a ritualistic, heavy emotional process when a loved one passed into a joyful state. However, the years went on and I became more human, so to speak, and more rooted in this lifetime with my emotions, personality, and age. I developed an understanding of death as a two-way street, seeing life and death as in a forever dance with each other.

Life truly wins because we came from the ultimate source of life in God, the universe, or the creator (however you look at it). If you don't think the creator can die, neither can you. You can be seen as a part of this creation or a co-element of this creator. That being said, there is a natural course of "emotions," which contains the root word "motions." Emotions are always in motion, and handling them is no different.

From my own personal practice, I have seen time and time again clients with high-risk behavior due to grief. Some are addicted to substances while others have suicidal, homicidal, or self-injurious risks associated with unresolved grief for a loved one. These individuals linger in painful emotions or stifle their pain throughout many years. Grief has truly no time limit without proper processing.

Many cultures stigmatize crying and do not honor emotional processing. I learned from being on the other side that there is an emotional part of ourselves in our souls that is just as real as any part of us here on earth. The grief and sadness that I went through in potentially losing my childhood, my parents, and, most importantly, what could have been was still carried over when I went to the other side.

I often say to my clients, "You wouldn't go for weeks, months, or years on end without going to the bathroom, brushing your teeth, or taking out the garbage, would you?"

They say, "That is gross. Of course not."

I then ask them, "So what are we going to do to address the emotional stuff hidden in your closet that keeps on causing the heartache, pain, and heaviness that is holding you back?"

Once we start to see ourselves as multidimensional beings, not just as a body that identifies what it can see with its physical senses as real, we recognize with deeper awareness the illusion of the body. I have learned to see physicality as a vehicle or reflection of the inner part of ourselves, a manifestation from our emotional, psychological, mental, and spiritual being.

Similar to the relationship of the mind and body that is still not well understood by science, there is a governing central point of the soul that influences our physical reality. As a result, I never personally or professionally recommend bypassing one's pain here on the earth plane.

Diamonds are made under pressure and so, too, is one's growth. One of the great gifts of grief is more empathy, compassion, and a space to hold and help another. If we are here to be our brothers' keepers, the burdens are opportunities in the big-picture perspective of the soul, allowing us to evolve, grow, and soar so that life here on the earth plane prepares us to be wonderful guides for others once we leave the physical body.

I often say that this lifetime is a preparation for the eternal marathon that we continue running when we leave this world. We can't expect to be up to par to run the marathon in only one lap. Through the personal growth that comes through situations of pain and grief of losing a loved one, our laps here on the planet can help open up a whole new world for ourselves and for our neighbors.

Part of what I learned through connecting to guides, angels, and others in my near-death experience was learning how to be a sacred observer. By that, I mean being one who is here empathetically and unconditionally without pushing a personal agenda. The sacred observer meets the moment in a raw form of pure understanding as if another person's pain were one's own.

The beings I met on the other side embodied this, encompassing a one-team outlook where no one is trying to get ahead but everyone is pursuing the same goal. I try to achieve this in my personal and professional lives, learning how to support others unconditionally within their evolution and growth on the earth plane. The loss of a loved one is an open, vulnerable wound. People are looking for answers that their loved ones are okay and that their nightmares of loss are not real.

I would suggest that when consulting or handling grief, the biggest issues are lack of empathy and the bypassing of pain. Some prefer to avoid thinking about the loss of loved ones and shut down emotionally. In bypassing, we hang onto the fantasy of what we want there to be by avoiding what truly is. I believe that one of the gateways of transformation is to go through it.

For me, I could not just get to heaven and cross over to the other side with a flip of a switch. I passed through a gateway within my consciousness due to the loss of physical sensation. I might have wanted to get to the other side without any pain or suffering, but I learned that the euphoria lay in going through the process of pain while recognizing its illusions.

In other words, the only way out of the experience was through it. Only then was I able to appreciate my own life, as well as all of the things I took for granted. I view grief as the same. We are never truly the same after losing a loved one, but in a way we can be more mindful of our own time here. After what we have been saddened by, we are able to carry on to make the most out of our lives.

Seeing in my NDE how instantly the life I had could be eliminated from the eyes of others, I learned very quickly the fragility of it all. However, I was more than fine and could go on. I learned then the value of giving yourself and your loved ones your best effort each and every day and living each day as if it would be your last. As long as we can strive for this, we will know that we did our best.

The vast majority of people can't say they are perfect, and unfortunately many episodes in our lives do not have a Hollywood ending. This often leads some of us to a lifetime of beating ourselves up through guilt. Many hold on to resentment for years and never allow an opportunity for forgiveness. Are souls angry at us, and should we be angry at ourselves?

I learned that while we carry our personalities into the heavens, we are there in a pure state of consciousness, forgiveness, awareness, and love. Loved ones in the heavenly realm embody pure forgiveness and understand the lessons learned through disputes. From the vantage point of heaven, both parties have opportunities to work out their problems and return back to what they are by removing the divisions that they are not.

For those on the earth plane holding on to grievances and riding out their normal course of bitterness and resentment, what if that course is breaking you, holding you down, and making life seemingly unbearable due to the pain and suffering it causes? Let a grievance instead be the cause of learning how to forgive yourself and love yourself, which will allow you to forgive and love another.

Love is what you are and what connects you to all. Awareness of that loving connection lights up your world. When there is a disconnection, darkness becomes a reality with a momentum that is contagious and equalizing to all it touches. The path of love begins with the decision that you do not have to do anything but honor and live out what you decide to give your power to.

One of the gifts that I gained from my NDE was the power to connect with loved ones on the other side. As I mentioned earlier, grief can be a huge weight when needing to hear, listen, and connect with those in the heavens. I've witnessed, however, the miracles of connection beyond the physical through firsthand and secondhand connection.

When considering an evidential mediumship reading, I would suggest doing your proper research. In grief, a "medium" can often prey on what you want to hear and take advantage of your vulnerability. It is important to go through someone who has been properly trained, tested, and is not grabbing information from you.

An authentic mediumship reading is quite the opposite and will use you as an echoing board of validation for the messages received. I have been blessed by several of these readings that have changed my life. Since my near-death experience, I have at times been able to connect to my loved ones who have crossed over. At times, I am my biggest skeptic and I question whether the information that I am hearing is a fantasy based on what I knew I wanted to hear or if it is an actual communication.

Based on my personal experiences, mediumship readings are helpful to validate what you hear personally. Specific messages and information that I received directly have been echoed in readings from evidential mediums. While it is important to be a healthy skeptic, I've learned not to question yourself to the point of having your hands in front of your eyes and ears. It has taken practice, but throughout my lifetime, I've learned to trust in my gut to discern what is coming from my head and what is from Spirit.

This skill is gained through practice and a developed ear, much like a musician. I normally communicate with loved ones as I am about to go to bed. This form of communication has no limit because they are watching me every moment and are not preoccupied or limited by their bodies as they were in their lives. I learned that losing a loved one is merely a change of shape and dynamic.

Part of what I have found through my own losses is the illusion of loss and how it can be a gain. So many struggle with the idea of noncontinuity, not only of loved ones after they die but also with a total cessation of rapport and relationships with loved ones in the physical world. For many, there is a stigma against interdimensional dialogue.

In the losses that I have had, there has grown a pure connection without any limitation to loved ones on the other side. From them I have learned validating messages of the euphoria they experience, including regained energy and reappearance of their youth. Connecting with loved ones on the other side in their passing, even if it is felt to be an imaginative conversation, can be helpful because it creates communication and processes feelings.

First, though, I would recommend working out the emotional part. I consider the last phase of grieving to be reaching a deep knowing that you and your loved ones are okay. This can be followed by a retrieving or evolving relationship with that loved one. To do this, the first step is key because you have to be in the proper state before the energy is possible for them to come down and for you to go up.

I think of the word "death" as synonymous with an ending. Throughout my experiences, I have learned of physical death as the opposite. It creates a new, transformative dynamic that can take whatever form you had before and expand to an even greater extent. In the following, I have designed a guided meditation that I use myself and share with my clients to connect to their loved ones, including family members and pets. It can be used to communicate with spirit guides, angels, and more:

> *Place yourself in your mind's eye on a beautiful beach on a warm, sunny summer day. Visualize the beautiful currents moving in and out. Inhale the beautiful air from the ocean breeze. Hear in the background the sounds of gulls in the distance.*
>
> *Position yourself on a beautiful beach towel. Feel above the beautiful sunshine shining on your skin. Sense the warmth, healing, and love radiating out of the sun. Look at the beautiful blue sky dotted with*

clouds in the distance. See the clouds moving slowly, peacefully, and effortlessly.

Allow yourself to take slow and deep inhalations. Inflate your core with pure divinity, awareness, and consciousness. Exhale and let go of any heaviness, sadness, anxiety, and suffering. Notice yourself becoming lighter, freer, and more whole with each breath. Take notice of the ocean waves crashing in on the shoreline and going out back to their source.

Life on earth is here for a short while, and we, too, go back to its shoreline. Allow yourself to expand in awareness, becoming one with the clouds, the radiating sun, and the endless sea ahead of you. All is well.

Notice in the background any family members, angels, guides, or pets who are walking in the distance. Just like the ocean water, flow with whomever and whatever comes in your way. Allow these beings to present themselves to you. Take notice of any words that you have for them and they have for you.

As you sit here, notice how proud they are of you in your life's journey and how they truly never went anywhere. Feel the love that always connects you with them. It can never be damaged, harmed, or broken. It is eternal, just as you or they.

Feel the love and allow yourself to take in a moment of joy, mutual embrace, and unity with your loved ones. When you are ready, you can take this feeling down through the top of your head and into every cell in your body. Feel it radiating in you, noticing that they were never distant. They are always there right by your side. Awareness just opened you up to these eternal bonds.

I hope you enjoyed this exercise. I have found it vital to process not only grief but the changes of life. Let it all flow without judgment or force. It is important to listen to the gut and follow its inner voice of healing. If you feel like singing, sing. If you feel like writing a letter, write one. There is no rulebook, guidebook, or chronology of healing or connection. Each and every person, passing, and connection is unique.

There are certain courses of grief, but I believe we are not here to suffer but rather to transform and evolve through the temporary passing illusion of suffering. What you had with a loved one is personal, and likewise the process of connecting to them should be made into a process of an inner personal experience and a journey of returning back to pure awareness and connection.

Grieve what calls for you. For some, lighting a candle is healing. For others, connection is maintained by wearing a wristwatch or a sweater of a loved one or going to their favorite restaurant and ordering their dish. Going through this process can allow one to open up to an even greater awareness and a deep, quiet knowing that nothing truly was lost. Within loss is the door to pure gain, connection, and unlimited awareness. The last step of the process is retrieving, evolving, and growing from what was lost in the mind but never in the reality of the heart.

Throughout our pain and suffering, we can recognize that there indeed is a light at the end of every tunnel, and the light that connects us all can never be broken.

Chapter Six: Uncovering Your Superpowers

You may believe that you are responsible for what you do, but not for what you think. The truth is that you are responsible for what you think, because it is only at this level that you can exercise choice. What you do comes from what you think.

—Marianne Williamson

As kids, we all had that one individual who we looked up to. Some took the form of a fictional character instead of a human in the real world. Marvel has a near cult-like following with children wanting to be their favorite superhero, such as the Hulk, Captain America, or Thor. Go to any Comic-Con event and you will see a mass following of people in this near-underground world dressed in the garbs of their favorite characters, often taking on their responsibilities. What is it about our culture and our obsession with superheroes and their special powers?

I had some firsthand awareness of this contemplation beginning at the tail end of my near-death experience when I was in the arms of eternity with its surrounding intelligence and guiding forces. There, I was summoned to one of the most profound lessons of my lifetime in the moment when I decided to return to my life and finish my chosen path.

As a human being, my maturation occurred nearly a decade and a half later when I was looked at as an adult capable of my own decisions. The governing forces on the other side look at children in an entirely different light of responsibility and certainly set a high bar of maturity and expectations. I agreed to stay on the earth plane with all of the lessons, pathways, and potential impacts ahead.

This decision came with a commitment to navigate all of this amid a return to human conditioning. It was understood that I would cultivate my inner knowing every day. It was with that decision that life began for me anew with a more profound outlook.

At that moment of choice, the spiritual forces slowly began to fade; not in a sense that they disappeared, but they were not directly in front of me. There was a knowing that they would never leave me. The best analogy I can give to any parent or loved one is when we are filling up gasoline, are we ruminating about how we love our children or loved ones? Just because we are not thinking of them does not mean that they are not present or that our love is lessened.

It would be quite intrusive and borderline concerning to think of our loved ones on a constant basis. Similarly, I learned that beings on the other side are like the stars at night. We don't always see them in front of us, or think of them all the time, but we know that they are always shining through us and with us.

It was not easy to remain in tune with this knowing. Vulnerability, anxiety, and the heavy sensation of doubt began to creep in when I stepped out of the light of my near-death experience. I went into a state of incubation between the two worlds where both light and the absence of its presence could emerge. A profound moment of inquiry occurred.

I wondered, "How do I know and trust that what was shown to me in my life path of helping others as a healer, helper, and workshop leader will be true? How can I be sure that my destiny is a guarantee and I won't have a life of heartache, deprived of this promise and diverted from my contractual agreement and vow?"

My spiritual guides were the only ones with me in these last few moments. My soul family members, angels, and loved ones were out of direct awareness and clear sight. The message that I received was, "Watch your thoughts because your thoughts influence your destiny."

My anxiety, doubt, and fear were transformed in those moments. At three, I was given a great gift to share with others on the inner powers. It was not just on the ability to connect to beings on the other side but how to direct the life that we were born to live. Slowly, my anxiety transformed to faith, trust, and empowerment.

Whenever I've felt stuck, I often remind myself of the great power that thoughts have. In my early adult and college years, I was uncertain of the path I was to take. This period prompted a rebirth from immersion in physicality toward a new outlook through spirituality.

During this quest, I noticed common themes from my guides and angels were now labeled and branded as *the law of attraction.*

I had no personal branding or words to describe the lessons from the NDE as they were tailored to my soul and not neatly summarized for an audience or a book. I was less focused on a catchy phrase but on the greater implications and versatility of the concept and the power of thoughts as a superpower in life.

Each of us has a unique life path. A distinguishing factor relates to the unique evolution of a soul through this school of life. The contrasting human themes of health, finance, family, relationships, and hardships are not meant to bring us further away from love, light, and expansion but rather are the fabric of their reality.

No one can tell us who and what we are meant to be. We are all mystical, eternal, and powerful beings. Our perceptions are an undeniable trait of strength and skill. We are already superheroes with unique gifts that transcend and surpass anything our imagination can conjure up once we take the time to sit with what is deep within. On our path to discover and use our gifts, our loved ones and spiritual guiding forces are always behind us.

How then do so many people forget who they are and what their purpose is? In a state of forgetfulness, how can we get back on track? I believe the current system inherently takes away our power. We tend to live from day one in a people-pleasing world. There are limitations in the dynamics of human love in the many times that we act to gain the approval of others. Within these limitations, we can easily lose ourselves in approval, chasing because what makes someone else happy can indeed be a betrayal of what is true to ourselves.

Whenever I've felt lost, the best solution I've found is to become aware of where or in whose hands I was putting my power. In general, if I was making choices to satisfy someone else, I wasn't being authentic to myself and my purpose. A big universal lesson in our society is to have stronger and unconditional love toward ourselves. Once we do this, it is easier to make empowered decisions. Even though these decisions risk potential rejection from others, they will come from our biggest ally at the end of the day.

Within the moments of my near-death experience, I fully understood how time and space were one. A thought that existed in that realm showed its great power and influence on destiny. From the vision that I had, I realized that I was not chasing something outside of myself in some far-out place years down the road. A thought of my soul's mission and plan already existed in reality.

On the other side, I wasn't in the process of potentially morphing into my future. I was already a teacher, guide, and sage. Here on the earth plane, I had to reconnect into that knowing of my true nature. So many people have what they may consider vague or impossible dreams. They delay or rationalize them away with the excuse of, "I will do it when I am ready." My near-death experience taught me that I was already there within my mission as a soul. Back on the earth plane, I had to put faith and trust in my visions, dreams, and destiny over limited, restrictive, and short-sighted limitations influenced by fear.

In this life, once I began to see these changes, my path was further influenced by the confidence that I was already the person that I was seeking to be. I realized that I was not an incomplete person who needed first to change to be that light at the end of the tunnel. Congruent with the theme of my NDE, I understood that here on the earth plane the light was within me.

Everything else, including fear-based doubts and insecurities, was just illusions. I have found that the more power we give to our visions, dreams, and desires, not only do we gain the confidence to pursue those pathways, but we attract what we are. This does not mean that the law of attraction or abundance hands our lives to us on a silver platter. Instead, confidence in our latent power aids us to navigate more easily through the process of the pursuit, including the pain. We can devote our lives to our highest goals when we realize that the biggest hurdle is often not the outer obstacles but the constant doubt that we place in front of ourselves and need to overcome.

The lesson of thoughts and their influence on destiny within my near-death experience paved the way to an unfolding and expansion on the lesson in this life. Our thoughts carry a great magnetic force field that tremendously influences everything. One of the biggest dangers that people face is rooted in the moment when they stop seeing themselves as multidimensional beings and forget their great power and great responsibility.

Just as we would not go every night to a buffet with toxic and high-fat foods, the same principle exists within our own thoughts and their influence on the lightness and heaviness of what we attract. The thoughts that we send out in words and manifest in our actions are as significant as the thoughts that we engage in our internal self-dialogue. These have a quiet but powerful influence on our self-identity.

Our view of who we are and what life is about influences the world that we see. Perception is indeed reality at the individual and collective levels. I firmly believe that we can influence the trajectory of this life based on our intention through the power of thought. Ultimately, each one of us has the duty to ask ourselves, "Is this thought or perception of myself bringing me closer to or further away from love?"

Within our culture, there is a constant pursuit of materialism in the form of various things. I always ask myself, what are people truly running to, and what hole are they trying to fill? Through the power of thoughts filled with unconditional self-love, I stopped chasing that need "to get there," to be somewhere or something, because I already am at that point.

Part of this life's purpose is not to morph into anything that we are trying to be or do. The thing that we are chasing is often temporary. It goes away completely or recedes into an ever further distance. So much of this lifetime is remembering who we already are. Our true nature is one of triumph, making us superheroes unknown to ourselves.

Our existence is not a maze of riddles to untangle or endless routes to get to a destination. From remembering our true nature and learning how to cultivate thoughts of self-acceptance and love, our destiny and ability to attract and live out our purpose becomes clearer. Then, the road ahead is not cluttered by the accidents of life and outer forces. We learn that no one is driving our car but ourselves. Part of driving skillfully is having a clear identity of who we are and what makes us happy. Once we are able to know and accept this, we will know where we want to go. This understanding makes it easier to ignore the naysayers and distractions on the side of the road of our journey.

In our society, taking control of our thoughts and cultivating them with loving intention carries a great responsibility. It takes effort and we may try and fail as we evolve on the path. There are many challenges. Throughout the day, we are conditioned in a world that passes judgment based on our job, relationship, or perceived management of our lives. Many of us can become enslaved by how the world views us, making it how we view ourselves. This puts the soul of infinite love and acceptance in dysphoria and separation from its true nature. This limited view of ourselves impacts our worldview for potentially a lifetime.

Once my brain shut down in my NDE, the entire world outside of my finite body shifted to a state of infinite grace on the other side. A lesson I learned was how we often get in our own way with our thoughts, perceptions, and limitations. I found benefit in my life from stepping back from my current thoughts and getting beneath them. I next set a conscious intention to release limited perceptions, recognizing that many thoughts are not my own but are inherited from someone else.

Once I am able to get to the root of my thoughts, a sensation of endless warmth, forgiveness, and nurturing emerges. This is the place of sacred timelessness and a reminder of all that exists. In those moments, my racing thoughts of illusion, often stemming from what others are chasing, can be seen for what they are. Thoughts that do not serve my own greater and highest good are canceled, and I am able to break free from a place of unconditional comfort. In that state, I recognize that who I am is enough. I also begin to understand how all of life is enough.

Having a clear connection to our true nature and disciplining our perceptions influences our thoughts and therefore the world. What we attract can be based in anxiety and fear, bringing more of the same, or intentional thoughts can open up avenues of empowerment. I believe that lessons related to the power of thought are repeated until they are truly learned and embraced.

The law of attraction certainly has influence in attracting different life scenarios but explaining tragedies or genocides like the Holocaust are when I believe it has its limits. Collectively or individually, are innocent people thinking about and deserving of such horrors? Some events, however gruesome they are, seem to be part of the individual and collective plan.

Nevertheless, understanding how the inner level relates to our outer experience can be a real ally toward understanding life's purpose. Whenever something is perceived as negative, I find a major benefit in seeing it through a different vantage point. A shift of perception changes the question from, "What happened?" to "What did I attract?"

This internal inquiry takes the situation deeper. Once we see life as a school to sharpen perceptions, there is a tendency to focus on making ourselves truly aware. We automatically tap into our power of being great attractors through the portals of our multidimensional being.

A consistent practice of doing this can help transform victimhood into opportunity and create enhanced wisdom after lessons are embraced. We all have the power to do this. This is the gift of creation that we have at all times, in all situations. My near-death experience taught me not only that there is so much more that we aren't aware of in the heavenly dimensions but that we as souls are so much more than we can imagine.

No matter what is happening in our lives, I believe thoughts contain the greatest freedom. It's helpful to remind ourselves of this on a regular basis. Many people are seeking transformational experiences in their lives. I find this theme within my work where clients want to experience what I have and even more.

While wanting to expand and grow is laudable, when people want more and more, this is an unfortunate reflection of the world that we were raised in with its constant urges, pursuits, and desires. Monitoring our thoughts and reminding ourselves of the great power within to maneuver through life helps us to understand that we don't have to chase after something spectacular or transformational.

We already have the power in our hands to change our lives based on how we perceive them. This prevents us from a constant reliance on the outer unpredictability of life. We do not have to wait for the unpredictable and chaotic external world to change in order to have an inner experience.

The power of thoughts has influenced me both personally and professionally. I have made it my duty to work with clients on cultivating this power. In my experiences, our culture of constant complaining, victimization, and a focus on the outer world is the crux of suffering. Similar to the unstoppable currents of the ocean, sometimes we need to allow ourselves to ride out the natural course of surface tidal reactions first.

In moments of despair, much like the moments of suffocation leading to my near-death experience, life can be brutal, but we must not let ourselves suffocate our own lifetimes. When we find a way to let go of suffering and our attempts to power through life's challenges alone, we open up to the grace of a higher love to guide us. Releasing control and self-limiting narratives is the most empowering act of all. When we remind ourselves that we are not separate from our source and that our lives do not play out in isolation, we learn to birth our lives and perceptions from a source that is virtually unlimited in its power.

I have learned that our destinies have multiple potentialities. Our lives are not set in stone. This lifetime stems from the ultimate source that we are all connected to. We take responsibility for our thoughts, perceptions, and the integration of the light within to shine as the light without. We have the constant choice either to be swayed by the constant trials of suffering or to return to the eternal fire within.

At times we can veer off the blueprint we charted with the divine, but life has funny ways of getting us back on track through highly unlikely circumstances and events. It is no coincidence that these happen. As the expression from Tolkien goes, "not all those who wander are lost."

It often feels like the trajectory of our lives is a massive responsibility that we don't know how to influence. How we perceive the journey and our connection to the source can create a deeper connection with our soul and its inner dialogue. Understanding the power of taking a daily inventory of our thoughts and the reality we are creating can truly be the bridge connecting our life to a sense of purpose.

It also assists in creating a flow of guidance, ease, and harmony with who we are and with our profound purpose. The thoughts emanating are the music that we send to ourselves and the world around us. Make sure every day to take notice of the vibration and sound we are playing and that this is a frequency of creation that represents our unique soul and its message.

Chapter Seven: Windows of the Soul and God

The spiritual journey is individual, highly personal.
It can't be organized or regulated. It isn't
true that everyone should follow one
path. Listen to your own truth.

—Ram Dass

What does the word "God" mean to you? The term itself is limiting because it is merely a word processed through the mind that conjures different forms of meaning.

As I'm sure you've noticed, I use this word throughout my story in order to be as flexible and vast in its verbiage as God itself. But I also refer throughout the book to Source, Love, and the Great Light as the dominant characteristics that offer a limited viewpoint of the divine. There is much more meaning, depth, and expression to God than even those aspects. From the standpoint of practicality, I will use the word God as an instrument of my best abilities to describe what I saw on the other side.

We are all aware of how the term God is subject to many degrees of use and interpretation. For some, the phrase "in the name of God" is spoken for the most sacred purposes. Others reference God as a force for power and conquest in holy wars such as the Crusades, where God backed those who claimed to represent "him" and his demands.

I grew up in the Jewish faith and tradition where God's name is rarely used or almost forbidden. In the Hebrew language of Jewish scripture, God's name is translated to *Jehovah*. Growing up, a complex reality was brewing inside of me. The God I connected to and knew on a personal level through my near-death experience was a totally different version from the God who was taught to me by my family.

In this, I don't see my life as all that different from anyone else's. Within each of us is a part that is connected to the divine. I believe we are breathed from the divine. Yet as we grow up, this inner connection seems to be lost and confused with cultural and religious programming that overtakes and erodes this personal and intimate connection.

I and many others in the Western Judeo-Christian world were taught an interpretation of God with human characteristics. It was a God who had emotions, punished, became jealous, and seemed to prefer one race, creed, and sect over others. Many who followed the word of God were praised as being "God-fearing," almost as if God were the great judge in the courtroom of life.

Within my religious background, there was a blueprint and guidebook to get closer to God. This was through the words of the Old Testament, which was believed to be the channeled word of God to Moses on Mount Sinai signifying God's hand in the Jewish exodus from Egypt. Through following a strict set of commandments and decrees, you either became closer to God or didn't.

Growing up, I had a tight-knit background within my own family and school-related structure. This involved endless rigidity of rules that some viewed as freedom but I saw as a continual prison sentence for the ultimate power and control trip of man. In anything from what I ate, to how I dressed, to the specific times to pray to God, there was a prescribed order. It became an obsessive, neurotic lifestyle for many.

Underneath being programmed from such a young age, there was a deep, inner connection that went beyond the rules of the God that I was being taught and grew a great disdain for. I was a bit of a rebel, but I kept it hidden as it was one thing to say that you disagreed with the tradition but quite another thing to say that you personally knew a different God outside of the tradition.

Many are mocked, ostracized, persecuted, or even killed for going against the grain of tradition in their connection of God. At the time, I would rather have been left alone. I was confrontational and combative, but not enough to blow my cover and give my soul over to the wrong hands that would simply not understand.

The connection to the divine is a unique gift that you are to make your own. I had known God as life itself. My own personal connection to God was something that no one or nothing could take from me. I hid this deeply within myself until I was let out of the bubble and discovered a new foundation of confidence to make the connection to God and my experience a solid foundation that was no longer held in secrecy.

The best way to describe the sensation of connecting to God in my NDE was taking a cord from my soul and plugging it directly into its source. I had a clear knowing at that time that I wasn't just coming home but was coming to the eternal Light that created me and gave me breath. It existed beyond time, space, and limitation.

In those moments with God and among the euphoria, I began to laugh and think of my classmates. Looking back, that moment was like Shirley MacLaine singing, "Holy cow! They'd never believe it, if my friends could see me now!" The human experiences considered the most climactic and overwhelming do not even touch the ankle of it.

Within those same moments, I did not see Christ as artistically depicted with long hair, sandals, and a staff but rather as that same vibrational, endless high. I felt uplifted, comforted, and greeted in those moments. At that time, I began to understand Christ along with a deepening consciousness of the divine.

Throughout my life on earth, I've noticed a certain rigidity and desire for monopolization and ownership of God, Christ, and ascended masters. It was almost as if God, the eternal sun of boundless understanding and compassion, was blocked out by humanity who tried to make itself and its wisdom take the place of God itself.

I grew up being taught a God that did not come from the soul but rather through the intellect and mind, a god in man's image who was said to be unlimited but was incredibly insecure, jealous, vengeful, and rigid. The inner experience of God throughout my life and through my NDE was in stark contrast to this outer representation and expression.

I was aware in my experience that everyone has a unique energy, life path, and level of understanding. I look at each lifetime as an opportunity to evolve, expand, and grow closer to the light and wisdom of God, not through the linear mind, but through the eternal avenue of the soul.

Through this knowing, we can hold on to our true nature of divinity. By doing so, we have the opportunity to create a world where spirituality works with humanity. All around us on earth, we see the sad results when humanity has little application of spirituality. In contrast, a humanity in tune with its spiritual nature can truly bring heaven down to earth. I think we are here to do this on both an individual and collective platform.

I had an awareness and clear sight of God in those moments when I crossed over, but the more mind-boggling element was to be taken out of time, space, and the linearity that we are accustomed to within the mind. To me, God is the great light, frequency, and beginning, middle, and end of it all. As a child, I used to wonder if God is the creator, then who created God? Where did this God come from?

I would often just bug out. While the soul has a knowing, once we start getting into our own heads, it works from a platform of beginning, middle, and end that is not even applied to God. This limitation, of course, does not stop and start with time but also in comprehension of judgment, forgiveness, and love. The analytical mind and our brains by their very nature are finite in both their duration and capacity to understand.

So then, what is God and how do we relate to it and come closer to it? For me, God in its purest form, expressed in the English language to my greatest capacity, is Love, Light, Giving, Vibration, and limitless, Euphoric Joy. For a second, I want you to not just gloss over those words that are thrown around even more frequently in the New Age than mainstream media outlets portray energies of fear. I invite you to take in those words both individually and collectively and allow them to speak to you and the depths of your being. So many spoken words are tossed around regularly, and we skim over them without reflecting on their meaning. Beyond those words, what is most important is a deep, inner feeling and knowing of God.

Within my experience, I understood that each of us is not only eternally connected to God but indeed we are all expressions, companions, and partners with God. I don't believe that one day God got bored and said, "I will make man and woman to keep me company." A god of that kind has a need and emotions.

Rather, I believe that the ultimate power and drive of God is creative light, expansion, and life itself. That sounds like more New Age jargon, doesn't it? Let me try to make this as simple as I can. When I had my near-death experience and was dying on my knees in moments of darkness, I not only received my life back in flesh but became aware of the eternal life and light that I was and am forever connected to.

I became aware each and every day that in similar moments, we all face darkness. Even when humanity goes far away from Light and into the vilest evil, that small part of us that is always present can be a lifeline to call upon Light. We have this gift in the capacity to see, feel, and create light within the absence of it on the earth plane. This is the reflection in many ways of the human experience as co-creating with the divine.

In a way, I believe that is what we are to do on this earth when we come here in various levels of awareness. Some are higher teachers, while others are more direct foot soldiers. We all fall and get up, constantly in a dance of the choices of life, whether to shine and remember our true nature or give power to blindness, forgetfulness, and selfishness.

I once heard a saying that life begins when the ego dies. I learned within my NDE that I was not my body, car, family, or religion. On the earth plane, I was experiencing those things, but in the bigger picture, my soul was never attached. My true eternal home was God, light, and eternal love.

From my experience, God is far beyond the comprehensiveness of anything that we are exposed to. I have found that to know and understand God is to not be more immersed in the human condition and lost within the spiritual condition, but the opposite. While I go forward in life chronologically, I am always anchored in the eternity of my NDE, the other side, and our true home.

Many abandon this view in their childhood when we are constantly taught within the rat race to move forward. We need to grow out of it; "stop being a kid and be a man." While chronologically we advance, the true voice and nature of the soul's origin, which was once close to us, is abandoned. With it goes our awareness of a divine connection to God and our purpose. God is then not something within us but a projected concept learned in the material form of a great power held within the trust of those who hold it.

At the age of three, I did not have much in terms of worldly accomplishments or achievements. I was a cute kid. My parents loved me, but that was about it. How then did I have this awareness and consciousness while many adults today struggle to maintain any part of it? I believe that the first step is to be empowered, connected, and rooted in our foundation.

When I experienced God and Christ in my NDE, it was not a signed, sealed, and delivered awareness of experience where I climbed the God Mountain and saw everything. Looking back, I have learned that we all are a part of the divine and connected to it on an individual basis.

Part of the human experience is to feel this within ourselves, expand on our connection, and see it within others. God was the giver of life when I was breathless in my NDE. My clear dependence on this life-force is a principle that I believe we are responsible for knowing on earth. I have learned that love is the true oxygen here. Love is the creative power ingrained in our nature to give to all.

The word love, much like the word God, is a term open to universal interpretation. Much like our awareness, an expansion of a sense of God can grow within our lives. Love—the unconditional love that God is—is a key highway to this eternal road. From person to person, unconditional love is subject to unlimited, unfolding interpretation.

This is not merely an interpretation through the analytical mind, which is one of the pitfalls of a dogmatic approach to God. In many ways we came here not to know unconditional love but *to remember that we are it* and cultivate it in our lives here. It exists not so much in our direct awareness but within infinite applications in our lives.

We are here to love, serve, and remember this love, just as Ram Dass would say. Everyone on their own level comes to know love. I believe great evolution in love happens when it is not only about what impacts me and people who like me and act like me, but what will uplift both the "me" and the "we." At a higher level, they are one and the same.

Through the darkness of the illusion of the body, through the seeming differences of race, political preference, religion, culture, and personality, we are all challenged. It is easy to see yourself and people like you and love them, but it's much more difficult to see those who are different from you and love them too.

Jesus gave his followers the difficult spiritual work to "love your enemies and pray for those who persecute you." Much like God is the unlimited source of love, we are to embody this and find a higher level of being in a core point of the nature of love beyond the superficiality and illusion of separation.

God is an unlimited awareness that is both personal and collective. I believe this consciousness is not one that we have to "do" or "become." We are forever connected to it. I believe life on earth is a giant play for how we want to express, celebrate, and understand God. The question is, does God become a limited interpretation in the process, leading to an "us versus them" antagonism, or is God permitted to be the ultimate, collective unifier who seeks to receive back what we were given, which is a sacred life?

Sacred life from my experience does not have much to do with the human perspectives of what the term "sacred" might mean. Instead, what I consider sacred is this opportunity to make whatever we were handed into an expression that brings us closer or further away from God. In my NDE, I learned that the greatest collateral that we bring with us is not measured in our bank account (although technically if we use our resources right, that can help), but in the evolution, growth, and awareness of the soul or eternal love that we all are.

It can be muddied here on a daily basis, and certainly outer stimuli can cover it up. In the next chapter, I will explain in detail how to take better, more mindful care of our spirit through meditation, just as you would take a finite thing like a car and get it washed.

People often ask me: Does God judge and punish people? I learned that if you believe that yourself, that is the consciousness and interpretation of God that you can choose to have and use, but it does not have to be.

When I connected to God, it was something so out of this realm of limitation. I think what is important for us to consider is whether the God that we seek to understand is of our human awareness or of the higher awareness that we are connected to.

If we think of God as eternal love and awareness, then our duty here on earth is to uphold this truth. I view hell as a consciousness not waiting for us necessarily in the afterlife but something that we experience in this life. A sense of guilt may make us hesitant to go back to God and the other side. However, I never felt judged and never felt a token-awarding conditional God who was a big boss man/woman. Rather, I experienced an eternal, unconditional, and supportive radiant warmth of love.

In my life review, I noticed that we feel, understand, and sense our actions from the perspective of others. We are no longer just the self but expanded consciousness and interconnectedness with everything and everyone. The souls who might have sinned are not punished but rather see pain that was inflicted in another and feel it, sense it, and know it as just a boomerang reflection of pain that we caused others and ourselves.

Beings on the other side and the divine do not judge or punish but rather assist, comfort, and nurture so we can understand evolution, expansion, and love through further opportunities in the karmic wheels of our incarnations.

Along with God and other controversial subjects, I have mentioned Christ. Throughout every talk and lecture that I provide, this seems to be one of the most debatable subjects. I have come to understand that many interpret spiritual awareness with ignorance, judgment, and a condescending know-it-all attitude.

I hope that is not what you feel in my writings; certainly, my family knows this better than I do. They will most likely tell me to read my teachings when I am misbehaving because I am human just as much as anyone. As I have grown older and matured within understanding, I have learned the value of no longer really debating. I do this not because it is draining, irritating, and deflating—it can certainly be all of those things—but because I firmly believe that it is not productive.

I am certainly open to and respectful of each person's interpretation of Christ, God, and their beliefs. Nonetheless, I have an understanding that a spiritual connection is not in the interpretation or monopolization of anyone. All of it is open to one's consciousness and degree of understanding. I observe, do not judge, and am respectful of the biblical argument, but I do not engage in banter or debate.

I am always willing to concede, admitting, "You won the debate; you are right, I am wrong." However, is there really a victory if one loses and another is embarrassed, shamed, or proven wrong? Who and what then is God if a solitary individual or group can call the shots?

Christ to me is a term that I use to represent an awareness or consciousness. There is an analogy for spiritual understanding evident in the infinite intelligence of the creation of the solar system. I view God as the great, life-giving sun and the planets as degrees of understanding and evolution.

I view certain teachers and masters within close orbits and connection to the inner light that shines onto them. To take the examples of Buddha, Mohammad, Moses, and Quan Yin, there are many higher levels of consciousness and understandings of God. We see Christ and Buddha as human beings whose expressions are on a very high level of the divine. These beings did not exist in a state of fear, possessiveness, or power-seeking.

They are stars within us, but sometimes we forget that the stars that we are looking at are composed of the same elements as ourselves. This is a lesson of empowerment to get in touch with our unique, eternal, and sacred connection to the divine. This is not solely held in another's hand but in our own. The question then becomes, how do we decide to express consciousness and divinity? How can we base the trajectory and patterns of our lives off ingrained wisdom?

We are alive for such a short time that our lives can go within the blink of an eye. I will never forget realizing the duality of the fragility of the human body compared to the eternity of the soul. I find contemplative time to utilize this limited existence. It can allow our roller coaster ride to pause so we can reflect on who exactly we are and consider the great ball that we are living on as it rotates around the sun in a solar system. We can marvel at how we breathe air through our lungs so millions of cells can work and how it was a literal miracle for one sperm out of tens of millions to make it to the egg, resulting in us.

Such deep thinking is not only helpful philosophically. It helps us be truly productive in the long run because we are not a money-driven machine at the end of the day. That cycle of need fades as quickly as it rises. Our true nature needs nurturing and to be reset on occasion to improve our intentions of expression and awareness in our lifetimes.

Gaining a sense of God within my NDE was not the end of my soul's journey, just like the loss of my bodily functioning was not the end of my life. It has become an everyday quest and drive within the ultimate life's purpose to expand awareness and cultivate it in daily living.

As my dear friend and colleague Peter Panagore says, "Dying taught me that death is just a beginning." Each and every day is an opportunity to inhale a higher consciousness and awareness of love and let go of old limiting patterns about the self and God. Our life is one big rhythmic breath of expression of God.

Chapter Eight: The Afterlife and Suicide

Earth has no sorrow that heaven cannot heal.
—Isaiah 35:10

My work in discussing my near-death experience has provided me with the distinct honor and position of working closely with those dealing with grief. By working with organizations that merge science and evidential mediumship, such as the Forever Family Foundation, and Helping Parents Heal (which works closely with parents in grief over their children), I encounter a lot of pain, suffering, and anguish.

Losing a loved one, I have found, is a very subjective matter where some grieve over losing a pet more than their own parent. It is natural to grieve in your own way and important to never judge how you are feeling. I am moved to see the gift of transformation from my own workshops and throughout the years working closely with evidential, accredited mediums and those going through their own loss.

I find it helpful that it does not change the empty chair on the holiday, or missing children throughout life events on earth, but for many it shifts to not having an empty presence of their loved one and having a new connection to them.

One of the most pressing issues that I find is losing a loved one to suicide, particularly losing a child. According to studies, suicide is the tenth leading cause of death, and each year there are one million suicides. Every forty seconds, a suicide is recorded. These are mind-blowing and heartbreaking statistics. When one commits suicide, not only is the loved one lost, but a death occurs with the surrounding family members and friends.

I encounter many in my workshops and in my practice who have lost loved ones to suicide. They experience intensified grief-related symptoms of anger, denial, bargaining, sadness, and most of all a sense of responsibility for the death. Many feel that if they had just visited the individual or said something or did something differently, then they could have changed the future. This is never more evident in parents, who tend to feel responsible for their child. They feel they have a sense of control over their child's destiny.

What then to do and how to view suicide from a higher perspective? Where is there to go when many internalize the feelings of suffering and endless pain that it leaves loved ones behind? Our cultural belief or set belief system poses barriers to looking at suicide from a higher perspective. The belief that someone needs to live a certain amount of time or that we are all the same on this conveyor belt of existence needing all of the necessary stages, ages, and set circumstances poses hardship to acceptance of suicide or losing one before their time. I do not believe that we can possibly measure chronological years, but rather it is important to look at the life within those years. One can live a very short chronological period but have an impact that can feel like eternity.

A major perspective that I have been able to internalize when it comes to suicide is to detach from cultural myth in chronological linear expectations of a boxed-in life expectance and to understand that we are truly spiritual beings having a human experience. We are not defined or limited by this human experience. In other words, our souls belong to a greater intelligence governing it before birth that is here for a journey that has no true beginning, middle, and end. Part of the issue with living in a linear world that many view as they see suicide as and ending but rather a part of a soul's journey, experience, and a new beginning.

I took several months off from writing *The Wisdom of Jacob's Ladder* when I was in the thick of creating this manuscript. I had hit a writer's block in the past, but this was something different. I kept on wanting to get back to this book, but something blocked me that I was not fully conscious of.

In September of 2021, a friend of mine made a decision and took his own body but not his life ... if you see what I am getting at. Ben had been a friend of mine who forever impacted my life. It was difficult as a friend to see his light decrease in front of my eyes.

Over the last few years, Ben had battled with his own mental health journey. Normally, my tall, blond-haired friend filled up a room with his personality and positive energy. But, in his last days before he chose out of this life, he wasn't the same at all. As a friend and therapist, I too felt an immense amount of guilt for his passing, thinking I could have done something or said something.

Within five minutes of hearing about Ben's passing while I was at work, I received a message from world-renowned psychic medium Jeffrey Wands, asking me to be a guest on a local Long Island radio station. In normal circumstances, I am the kind of person who never turns down events. I know how important they are to support my practice, and I love connecting with new, like-minded people.

But that day, I just had to sit down, barely seeing Jeffrey's email. I was in such a state of shock from the news that I told Jeff that I needed some time to process what had just happened with Ben.

I was able to be on Jeff's show two months later and ended up having a blast. By that time, I could be present and enjoy being an honored guest to talk about higher consciousness. It really affirmed that the world was waking up to a possibility that there is more to life than this.

During the radio show, the switchboard went out of whack and flickered erratically. I made a joke to Jeffrey, echoing what many near-death experiencers find: people like us tend to have an impact on technology. He looked at me in a direct way and said, "It's not that. This is directly related to you."

I stared back at the medium, not sure what he meant. Moments later, I understood.

Unexpectedly, Jeffrey added, "Your friend Ben's energy is here. He's making such a strong presence that it is impacting technology."

Slowly, I nodded. We are all electromagnetic energy that can never be destroyed. When we go into the afterlife, we carry our energy that has the capacity to impact technology in the most undesirable situations, at times such as being in a radio studio. Jeffrey went on to say that Ben wanted me to let go of the guilt that I was feeling.

"That was his path and his decision that you could not change."

I sat back in my seat as a profound truth hit me at that moment. Instantly, after hearing of Ben's passing, he was already at work as a guide to help me. He helped facilitate the connection to be a guest on Jeffrey's show, but also to present a message with one of the world's most respected psychic mediums to let go of my own guilt and responsibility.

That was a message that not only I needed to hear, but Jeffrey's viewers did as well. It is important to let go of a sense of control and ownership over a loved one. Our love for one another can make us smother and intensely care too much; this makes us want to forever hold and prevent any form of pain and suffering for a loved one.

The truth, as Jeffrey mentioned, is that no matter what we do or say, people have their own path. We can try to hinder it, but when there is a will, there is a way from either end of the spectrum. I asked myself weeks later how I could turn Ben's passing and death and give it a voice.

I use this as a prime example to showcase that there can be a purpose found within loss when the foundation is solid. Understanding that loved ones do not belong to us but rather are forever a part of the eternal spirit realm as infinite beings for different missions and experiences allows a sense of trust and knowing that we can let go of our pain. They can never be taken from us and are forever connected to us.

My friend Ben, like many souls who go down his path, learned from his own experience here. He was able to already help us here on earth and reach families in need of support. I look at loved ones as having callings even when their bodies die and their missions on the other side as reflective over themes to continue to learn, grow, and aid. Loved ones in satellites in heaven work closely with matters of their own lifetime and are here to create healing and evolution from learning from their own decisions.

Suicide for many can seem like a weakness, a cop out, or betrayal in life. In reality, to many who grew up with these lost loved ones, it can be seen in the exact opposite light. In my experience with Ben and others I have experienced, many who make this decision are some of the strongest souls to be able to have lived day in and out carrying their pain. This is a statement I often hear time and time again from friends and clients of when it comes to souls who are struggling and those who crossed over due to suicide.

Many judge the end result of someone's life as the sum total without really understanding their own unique mission and purpose here that comes from an infinite intelligence far greater than our understanding. Many carry weights so heavy to lift that they can cause life to be almost unbearable; it dims the lights of even the strongest. Is it weak to collapse when you have such weights tying you down? Is it selfish to do so?

For many suffering with these unseen challenges, it can be a daily grind just to stay upright and alive. I found it helpful to hear that perspective from a father who lost his daughter; it doesn't have to be a place of judgment or shunning, but rather a place to let go to see strength in all that they were able to endure day in and out.

Many clients who I have encountered recently are concerned about the judgment placed on their loved ones who have chosen out of this life. In my first book, *Life After Breath,* I shared about a previous life of mine in which I took my own life after hitting a wall on all cylinders. That past life experience at times crept up on me during my childhood. I often saw the same scene of people around me discouraging me to not do it and killing myself in front of others.

I became emotional during my NDE after re-experiencing that lifetime and connecting to my own students. I often experienced after the moment that I took my life in my NDE and in memory that I did not elaborate on in *Life After Breath* was coming back to the light just like any other carnation.

I was not judged, ostracized, or crucified. I think it is important to understand that we are in God's image and to take our own cultural viewpoints away from our image of God. In our society we judge, punish, and get angry. On the other side, we have emotions and an adjustment from the lifetime that we lived in incubational periods but are surrounded by infinite light, love, and acceptance of the divinity that we are.

The other side does not view one life decision as the end, nor does it believe in punishment. It looks at us in our infinite, eternal nature, as we are a soul experiencing another dimension of life so that it can remember who we really are.

I was able to understand the correlation between having my NDE as part of my karma or story, which I later transformed into my purpose of remembering who I truly was as an infinite being, with infinite love inside of me and around me that I could never be separated from despite any pain that I endured.

The moments after I took my life in the past, I was able to see that I would be okay had I turned in another direction. Plenty of people face the wrong direction in their lives for the resources of their lives on the outside. The outside world is filled with uncertainty, unpredictability, and suffering as many are facing the wrong way in their lives.

After seeing my last lifetime, I knew that if I shifted my viewpoint of my own suffering toward looking inward, I could remember that all that I ever needed, wanted, or desired was forever eternally connected to me. I did not need anything from this life, but it was here to experience growth, evolution, and spread the inner world to the outer world.

Many forget who they truly are, and it is a simple change of degree from living life from a place of lacking on the outside and to shift it from the inside outside. Life for many can feel soulless, which is why no wonder so many feel dead. I truly believe that many who commit suicide are not trying to die as on a higher level and subconscious basis they know on a deeper level that they can never die. They are wanting to live and kill the heaviness blocking them from living while they are living.

Souls who complete suicide from my own experience do not sit in a place of suffering. There is a healing that takes place and coming back into an understanding of what they experienced so that they can learn. Many identify the screen of their life without remembering the light behind it. It is important to remember that light is the GPS of our own light and true compass to navigate our reality.

I remind others of the simple message that they should not allow the world to influence their souls and minds; rather, they should allow their souls and minds to influence the world they live in. People who cross over after suicide certainly have important work to do. I believe that we came here for an experiential level. The lives we live shape and evolve our being.

For instance, I can research and talk about swimming until I am blue in the face, but until I actually get in a pool, it is a whole other set of criteria. I think the same goes for any incarnation and major themed experience. We are here when we cross over to be present in the lives of others to help evolve a theme that we went through so that others can evolve themselves back to awareness.

The moment that I was able to find a purpose was the moment in which the pain and flashbacks of that past life of mine started to go away. At times, difficult experiences feel like they are writing your story and taking over your identity. Remembering who we are not can be a great gateway to remembering who we are.

A month or two after my friend's passing, I began to get a flood of contacts from parents who had lost their loved ones to suicide. I firmly believe that our loved ones to whom we connect and with whom we experience a painful experience use us for our purpose. The soul has a contract with loved ones, and whether here or on the other side, we are teammates for life. The work never stops; it just heightens.

I wondered why I stopped writing my book. I knew on one level that I experienced a great suffering in the loss of my friend. Two months after his passing, I did a gallery event with a friend of mine, evidential tested medium Shelby May. She did her readings, and I gave a talk about higher consciousness at a local yoga studio. I try to arrange many events around Christmas and Hanukkah, as many experience heightened grief, loss, and pain from having the empty chair.

In working with mediums and sharing my NDE, the goal for the loved ones is to reframe that empty chair to not mean an empty presence and to know that our loved ones and life continues life itself. During the gallery reading, Shelby turned to me and told me that she was connected with my friend Ben. I politely declined as I wanted to make sure everyone else who was there could get all the time in the world for their readings.

Shortly after the event and escorting participants who received healing messages and a burning summer in the cold December air, Shelby turned to me again.

"Your friend told you to not stop writing your next book. He wants you to continue."

Shelby had no idea that I had stopped writing, and I just stared at her in awe and respect.

"He's guiding you in the book," Shelby continued, "and you had a delay because there was a message that he wanted to have. Had you not taken the pause, this message would not have been put in the book."

Thanks to Shelby's intuition and what I already knew in my heart, I know my friend wanted this. Our work does not die when our bodies go; instead, it actually amplifies. I believe when we focus on pain, we see pain. When we allow ourselves to go through our own pain in its proper time and to recognize all as a part of a higher purpose, we are able to transform the purpose of pain itself.

Death is the most universal experience that anyone can have. No one has defeated physical death of the body and physically lived forever despite being an internal being. Yet it can be the most paralyzing, lonely, and isolating experience that one can have. I have found that there is great benefit in getting support for your own grief, to know that you are not alone in suffering, and to receive when you are ready a place of healing, support, and guidance.

As always, be careful with whom and in what you place your vulnerability, as some can look like a wolf in sheep's clothing. Knowing that love never ends is just as important as honoring our emotional grief response. That process is a human thing since our souls know no end. It's important in this lifetime to acknowledge this grief like a wave in the ocean; let it pass through, without fighting it, and honor any messages that it may bring from a higher awareness.

When losing a loved one in any way, no matter how enlightened you feel or how much you know that they are there, it is important to not judge yourself. Jesus, who knew the kingdom of the afterlife more than anyone, cried when he knew that Lazarus died. Before he even got the news, despite knowing Lazarus would be alive again in moments, he still cried. He knew that just because death is not the ending does not mean that you cannot cry at sad moments. What a beautiful, gentle reminder to be kind to yourself and to honor the human part and emotional experience of life and to not judge the experience.

There have been many documented suicide survivors who have had near-death experiences. Through their own stories, they have had a firsthand encounter of God. Many, like myself in my own past life, tell that they did not get judged for the life that they lived. They understood with more clarity their own purpose. They remembered who they were and came to a life that felt more connected and spiritual, like other near-death experiencers.

It is my belief that a god with infinite intelligence cannot judge, blame, or get angry at its very self. We are all expressions of divinity in this sacred filum that we call life itself. Near-death experiences allow one to go from one spectrum of the rubber band of being a spiritual being having a human experience back to their own nature as a spiritual being back to the human experience.

Many, including myself, have come back with not a profound transformation in many ways on a deep level, but an integration of the core of our inner beings to be reinvigorated in life itself. People who attempt suicide and come back in their near-death experiences exemplify that even if they tried to, they could never die or be judged for their acts. Those who come through in the afterlife group together are on a mission to remind others that they have internal light and infinite strength to handle the struggles in front of them.

Many ask me that if we go back to an all-loving God, why not just complete this life if things become difficult? This is a profound question. I learned from my last suicide attempt in my previous incarnation that we are not punished; the only way out is through in many ways. We are here to transform a period of pain into purpose. The work never dies, and many who help out on the other side to assist with suicide come back to complete and implement what they truly know in life experiences in different sets of circumstances when they reincarnate.

Technically, yes, suicide is not painful, but it does leave pain for loved ones. When I took my own life and I entered the light realm on the other side, I was also upset at myself for forgetting that I was infinitely guided and protected beyond comprehension. Many with suicidal ideations have blinders on in deep depression and do not want to see anything else or believe in anything else beyond that stuck energy of suffering. My experience told me that suffering is real in this life, but in the relative it is an experience that can bring us back to who we are from experiencing what we are not.

When Ben passed, I began to work closely with Helping Parents Heal. I learned of the organization started by Elizabeth Boisson, whose son passed from severe altitude sickness at the base camp of Mt. Everest in Tibet. Moments later, Elizabeth felt her son's love, energy, and warmth and had a knowing that love never ends. This inspired her to start Helping Parents Heal, which assists thousands of grieving families and individuals on a global scale.

I have noticed how transformative the knowing that we are loved and surrounded by infinite light can be to the participants. I highly suggest if you or a loved one lost a family member to suicide or death that you journey forward in the proper steps and stages.

Consult with a reputable psychotherapist, and when there is a readiness, join a grief support group that addresses this feeling from the ground up. I know my friend Robert Ginsberg, who lost his daughter to a tragic car accident, started the Forever Family Foundation, featured on Netflix's *Surviving Death* series. He mentioned after the passing, while he attended grief groups, the participants would discretely meet up in the parking lot after the meeting to discuss signs and symbols from loved ones in afterlife communication that were not allowed to be discussed while in the grief group.

Based off this observation, he thought why not create a group that allows and highlights this phenomenon in a safe way. He and his wife decided to start the Forever Family Foundation, which has now become internationally recognized. It is a wonderful group that highlights afterlife consciousness, science, and evidential spirit communication to support loved ones in their grief. Organizations like Forever Family and Helping Parents Heal are incredibly helpful, as they allow grieving loved ones to utilize afterlife phenomena to cultivate the knowledge of a presence of their loved ones in everyday life.

The common messages from attending gallery readings and my own evidential readings when it comes to suicide speak to letting go of responsibility of death. My dynamic with Ben is a microcosm of how they also want us to grieve. I find it helpful to give the most voice and life to what we see as the voiceless in our reality. Finding an organization, support system, or mission allows many like Robert, Elizabeth, and countless others to not only just know that our loved ones are okay but to be kicked in the butt and to have continuity of the life that they lived.

As long as we are telling their story and finding meaning, purpose, and a call to action, their death was not in vain. The impact is indescribable on all those who did not hear it. Christ was not the only one who went on the cross and suffered to remind us of our eternal life. Christ would speak like many masters that what is inside of me is always inside of you.

Loved ones suffered not in vain but in purpose in their own suicide. From looking at death itself, they were reminded that they are eternal life with a purpose far greater than our own pain. We are connected in our pain but also in the collective purpose of soul groups and missions. It is my hope that you can continue to write the chapters of their story just like Ben reminded me to in this very chapter.

Chapter Nine: Eternal Summer

When one door of happiness closes, another opens; but often we look so long at the closed door that we do not see the one which has been opened for us.

—Hellen Keller

I was sitting in solitude and gathering the peace of Long Beach, New York. The beauty of this beach on the south shore had a bit of a buzz to it and the energy of the population while meeting the deep serenity of the Atlantic Ocean. It was the end of August, early in the evening. The clouds were going down, and yet there was still a glimmer of summer that all the participants at the beach seemed to be grasping on to. I thought to myself that I didn't want this summer to end and let it go. Why can't it always be summer?

I have always gravitated to the warmth. Under the sun and by the ocean was where I felt most at peace. They seemed to wash away any fear that I had in my mind, as well as make myself and my problems seem dwarfed compared to the expansiveness of the ocean.

I heard of celebrities going into outer space, such as legendary actor William Shatner and his space travel. He became emotional when going up to space, realizing how small he saw the world was and how it put into perspective himself and the vulnerability of life and how small our planet earth looked in the atmosphere.

I have the same feeling when I go into nature. It seems to soothe as well as help me gain a vantage point of perspective to decrease the small problems that I create into larger ones.

I sat in a deep state of meditation, enjoying the sea salt air, warmth of the fading sun, and the faint noises of children playing in the background. I just wanted to hold on to that moment forever. The truth of linear reality here on this earth started to hit my idealism, and it got darker outside. I knew I'd at least try to hold on to this eternal moment of external and internal peace while it slipped out of my control.

The end of summer at times felt to me like the wicked witch was taking out her sand timer and I was there on the sand of the beach for every last moment. I decided to have a radical acceptance of the situation and slowly walk away while taking a piece of every last drop of the summer, the beach in my heart.

I decided to pay a visit to my grandmother, who lived one town over. My grandmother always reminded me of a female version of Fred Rodgers. Her warmth and sweet approach, yet sage, nonjudgmental advice was always something that I gravitated to. At ninety-seven, she was in tune with what really mattered and was always interested in the heart of what I was going through. She was my own sage therapist.

As soon as I arrived, she asked about my well-being, and I informed her that I was doing well.

But then she looked at me a little closer, with concern on her face. "Tell me, what is wrong?"

I sighed and took a breath. "Well, Mama," I responded, "I am doing okay but I am really upset that summer is coming to an end. I always have a hard time with that."

"I understand," she said with a nod. "You know, I have been on the planet a lot longer than you, and at ninety-seven I can tell you that no matter what happens or how difficult the winter is, the warmth always comes back."

I took her statements into my heart, considering them deeply. Within those moments, that same, eternal stillness and sensation of wisdom allowed its beauty to present itself.

I took it in and thanked her with a long embrace. I thought long and hard about it and started driving my car. I did not feel like listening to the radio but wanted to breathe in and marinate what she told me. It seemed that my grandmother always said the right message as if she was living in a place between two worlds at her stage of life connected to this side while also a part of a higher awareness from the other side.

I wondered why that statement "the summer always returns" was hitting me so hard. I was then given a moment of clarity to allow this beautiful message to come to me. It was the inverse of the sun going down earlier at sundown on the beach a couple of hours ago.

This felt as if in my mind's eye the sun of wisdom and guidance was filtering itself into my own consciousness and awareness. I began to hear and feel a message permeate my being. Much like my grandmother was referring to, no matter how dark the season or winter, it always returns. I thought to myself how brilliant of a statement that was in reference to this life as well as the afterlife.

I have always been taught that life is an earth school. I do not think that we have to necessarily learn anything as a part of the soul or our own superconscious. It is all knowing at its core, but we are here to integrate and apply the wisdom of who we really are deep down in this human experience. In reference to the earth school and the lesson of eternal summer, I was able to receive the messages of this analogy on a deeper level.

Have you ever had that difficult year in high school, college, or graduate school when going through finals? Eventually you pass the end of year exams, and you have freedom and a whole summer to enjoy. Part of you is in such disbelief. You think, *oh, no more tests, tension, or cramming!* You almost do not know what to do with yourself since part of your identity felt like it was permanently tied into and stuck to your experience in school. All of a sudden, you do not know what to do.

Your mind goes on autopilot, switching from going one hundred miles per hour in your studies to going to zero and almost creates anxiety in those days as having no worries or activities to do is almost foreign.

I linked this concept of the earth school and our experiences here to when we cross over. The summer is always there regardless of how difficult the winter might be. Much like the four seasons here on earth go through their natural cycles to balance mother nature, so, too, do we within our lives. Each season is here not by random but to further evolve and expand our own being.

If we had the sun in front of us all the time, we would sit on the beach all day. Now there is nothing wrong with this; we can do it someday within this life and the hereafter. It creates more strength and resilience when we are able to connect to and create our own life in, at times, the absence of it.

I was deeply taken by the writings of philosopher Albert Camus. One statement that he made that really speaks to eternal awareness of the summer within any moment is referenced by this: "In the midst of winter, I found there was, within me, an invincible summer. And that makes me happy. For it says that no matter how hard the world pushes against me, within me, there's something stronger—something better, pushing right back."

In my own personal life, it is when we go through moments of darkness when we allow our inner light to really be tapped into and utilized. I find that much like a mother when she sees her child trapped under a car or in a crisis, she is able to utilize her own instincts and adrenaline to save a child in what makes her out to be a superpower.

Our own true nature and our infinite awareness, however, may be buried and can show up in the most difficult moments. What is needed is to fine-tune the ability to understand to let go as a pathway to receive. Within our culture we are taught that our identity is defined by what we own and hold on to. Within the expansion of spirituality and consciousness, it works in the exact opposite.

This is because what is inside of us is all that we are looking for. Within us is what you can call part of the mind of God, or seed of wisdom deep within. Trusting our ability to listen will allow us to hear the guidance and allow the crack of light to come in and shine itself onto dark moments.

When working with clients who are going through moments of intense grief, crisis, and hardship, it is those exact moments of friction in life that lead to a whole new rebirth. Much like storms in nature or the dead of winter, these are moments that are part of the cycle of our own evolution.

I learned that what saved me in my NDE was not my body miraculously getting oxygen but connecting to the infinite true breath surrendering and letting it guide itself back into my own body. I believe that in moments of crisis or darkness that what is needed is more trust—a trust that our difficult moments were not there to break us. We have the ability to trust and surrender to the eternal Light within to navigate those difficulties.

We think of ourselves as our limited minds and personalities, but this is where I think people get into trouble. The mind itself is finite and limited. What is needed in crisis is tapping into and surrendering to an infinite intelligence that is deeply inside of us and connected through us. It is through indeed letting go where our biggest point of resilience and healing comes into play.

Going through this life as an experience with connectedness to greater purpose is vital to gain strength. It is hard to go through with any challenge not trusting what you are going through. Our capacity to see the other side of the hill and the importance of trusting in the process is the key. Much like in school, we can bang our heads and yell at our teachers, but what is in front of us does not change.

Part of the navigation of this earth school and a point of reference to remember is to trust in the infinite intelligence providing the assignments, the strength within ourselves to manage, and the ability to recall that what we are going through has a purpose (and an even greater purpose for our ability to find purpose within it). There can be two students in life: one who is constantly wanting for summer to come to an end and gets upset when he or she returns to school... or one who is in the moment and finds that light within situations.

I recognized that I needed that bit of truth. I remembered my grandmother's message that the summer will come regardless of any situation. So, too, will our own afterlife, and it will be a great, big reunion with our loved ones, friends, soul family members, spiritual guides, and helpers.

What is important to remember is to trust that we don't need to die to experience the afterlife or the infinite summer. It is not only something that we will experience one day but something that we can find in ourselves and something that at our core being we truly are. In the human experience, one does not need an NDE or shared-death experience to find it. In fact, it can happen in the smallest things or even the biggest struggles, as it is all within.

From looking at light we will see it, and in looking through darkness we can remember it. The summer always returns and is always a part of us, even within the dead of winter. As beings that are here coming from a summer break in this earth school, keep that light at the end of the tunnel and the light within.

The ultimate happiness I have experienced is not a transactional checklist where you hold your breath or lose yours like I did to find it. It is within the breath, the moment, and can be found in all things. All things at their core are infinite divinity, pure joy, and love.

Chapter Ten: Knowing of the Afterlife

There is no need to go to India or anywhere else to find peace. You will find that deep place of silence right in your room, your garden or even your bathtub.
—Elisabeth Kübler-Ross

"Do you believe in the afterlife?" is a common question that seekers ask when searching for answers when it comes to all things. The root of belief, however, is a different angle when it comes to higher consciousness. Our world is governed by our own beliefs from politics, religion, and identity. The issue of belief is that it is paradoxical when it comes to the afterlife and higher consciousness.

The near-death experience that I had was based off direct experience, which I refer to as a "knowing." It was, therefore, this knowing that I based my life on. Part of the issue is that many of the beliefs that we govern our lives by are inherited from the outer construct and influence by others. This can lead to many issues as they are not based off a foundational prism of truth, but within the degrees of separation from truth itself.

We therefore are only as good as what we are taught within reality, and this becomes our prism. It is no wonder why within humanity, when we step back from it, there has not been a needle that has been moved. Beliefs, like traditions, get passed on from generation to generation. How and where can it stop?

The answer to progress does not lie outside of ourselves but within our own backyard. We are not sole creations of this lifetime and the identity that we shape from it. Within ourselves is a beautiful awareness of infinity. We forget this as we have often been taught that we are separate from others and have our own sense of identity.

This separate notion has led to a "me versus the we" and an "us versus them" mentality. Our political identities have taken over our true spiritual ones. What we have been conditioned to become in this life has taken over the wisdom within.

Our beliefs will shape and influence the trajectory of the world. What is important to understand is that this life and world that we are living in is not something outside of ourselves or separate but rather an energy that we are a part of. Each person, when they reach toward a deeper, inner connection, influences a shape or different current within life itself. We all have a light within us that can illuminate the world. Darkness cannot exist with light present. The light does not turn on by itself but rather by each soul. The soul does not have to be lit but rather reminds itself of its true, eternal flame.

Many struggle with infinite consciousness as they put pedestals on others. The term "immortals" is often reserved for others who we see as godlike. We forget that the same thing that we see in an immortal or in God itself is inside of us too. There we can find the same eternal DNA.

From this awareness we can shift from unimportance to truth outside of ourselves to dig deeper and live an embodiment partnered with wisdom and opportunity. Life then becomes a sacred experience from viewing it from the mind and eyes of God within each and every one of ourselves.

When we have intimacy and connection with God, we see it within ourselves. We have the ability to evolve what was taught as separation to unify within an even greater consciousness. The root of belief is therefore a root cause for so many problems. It can be dangerous as it can be manipulated and controlled by humankind and limited filters. Many, in fact, who are devout to Christ's name have more in common with the oppressors of Christ than Christ himself.

I recognize many have been programmed to create their own world instead of their own mind creating and influencing their world. Their minds were not solely theirs but part of the thoughts and mind of God. Many forgot this and were not living a life connected within their own energy to a God-filled and connected life.

Life on the other side taught me that heaven did not belong to a set of circumstances; it was not a job application or a trial of pass or fail. In our world, we process things linearly, and that often leads to a black-and-white type of thinking of good and bad with no in-between.

The nature of our lives is often governed by anticipating future events and desired outcomes. When this or that adds up, then we will feel good. The viewpoint of conditional happiness and emotional status often governs our lives. The afterlife and other side operate on a much different construct. I learned in my NDE that as good as the afterlife is, it does not have to be after.

We do not have to leave our bodies to connect to peace, bliss, and expanded awareness. It can be found from having what I call a mind of heaven and eyes of God. We don't need to have heaven as a destination that we wait for. Our lives are connected to it. It is therefore liberating as on the outside it may not look like paradise. Paradise or our state of mind have nothing to do with the actual events but from the filter through which they are processed.

Living from this place does not change the events or hardships of the outer circumstances. There are days when I wish I did not have to toil in the physical world and sweat here with challenging ups and downs. No matter what we do, no one is immunized from the human experience. No matter how transcendental my NDE was, I still had to come back to living a life no different from others on the surface.

I try to find moments where I can see the godliness even in the difficult or little things. It is seeing the smile on someone else because of my smile or telling the bank clerk how much they are helping you. At times we all can get caught up in the human journey and its hardships.

Living a spiritual life does not immunize us from going through all of these steps, but rather it allows one to see the sacred in the mundane. Through this God-lens, we can see the beauty in all despite what is presented at face value. Depth sees depth.

The knowing of the other side and of consciousness is a full-time embodiment of it. It is not something to aspire to or wait for, but a recognition of this life as purposeful, meaningful, and part of one's inner journey of continual transformation through experiences. We at times seek to experience beautiful moments when we have time to ourselves and separate ourselves.

As I am writing this, Thich Nhat Hanh, an ambassador of peace and a monk, transitioned at ninety-five years old. He completed a chronicled run as a beacon of light and wisdom and lived a life that embodied an inner knowing of his divinity through mindfulness and actualization of higher awareness.

I read once that someone asked him, "How do I have time for myself when I am busy with so many things?"

He responded, "Why are you separate from those things that you are involved in? Are you not in those things no matter how small you label them? Why wait to get time to yourself when you can do it and be present at all times?"

I fully agree with this principle that we all can have an inner knowing that we are not here to live a life on cruise control, disconnected from our lives, but that our spirituality comes from our ability to be present.

When I crossed over to the other side, there was a presence of ultimate presence. Time fully stopped. I looked at the other side through a sense of familiarity from being there in other previous, in-between lifetimes, but there was a sense of timelessness in which an endless presence existed. It was full awareness.

We all have the possibility to let go of what we have been taught in order to embody who we truly are and the infinite wisdom inside of us. We do not need a guru, teacher, or outside force. There are those who can help guide us by walking beside us, but those kinds of mentors do not create what has always been inside.

This is a contrary trajectory and principle to what we have been taught. The difference of belief versus knowing is belief has a possibility, clinging to a destined set of circumstances. Knowing is an unwavering awareness, much like asking someone if he or she believes that the sky is blue or simply knows it is. Deep down, we all have an inner knowing of truth that is in our own backyard.

You can get high off the concept of enlightenment, but if it is not integrated in a way or used for daily contact, it becomes a great unread fantasy novel on a bookshelf. We are the seed of eternity here to grow our seeds and nurture others. Embodying, knowing, and remembering this eternal seed can open up a window to our responsibility to take care and nurture our soul family here in this life.

At the start of this chapter, I posed a question: Does the afterlife exist? I think not. Our beliefs are limited and held within information outside of ourselves. We have the ability to remember. The moment that my brain stopped working through suffocation during my NDE was when I connected and remembered who I was.

I learned that our own memory is far beyond the creation of our own brains.

I view the brain as the filter of life but not the final creator of it. When someone asked me as a young child if I believed God existed, I drew a blank. This individual would give me all of the scholarly religious texts in existence and all of the typical, rational arguments. These can help, but to me God is actually an irrational thing. It is irrational as it is beyond the linear mind and its processing, and far beyond the filter of our five senses.

It is much closer and deeper to us; it is within our souls and the breath of it. I firmly believe that the afterlife and God exists within ourselves and all things. We are forever connected to the afterlife, and the afterlife is connected to us. "We are one" is not just applicable with our brothers and sisters in physical forms but within all forms. This is the mind of heaven, the one that does not need to be transformed to be awake. It's inner awakened awareness in a dreary world creates a transformed world.

I am thankful for my near-death experience but do not wish it on anyone. It is a great gift, one that I live my life by, but my experience in my soul is not a sole experience but an experience to connect and impact other souls. Christ died on the cross, and many NDE-ers are Christlike for their own experienced physical trauma. Often, those torturous physical moments only remind them of the doorway of recollection to their true, infinite nature, where they have seen pain as a temporary experience but a long-term illusion from the vantage point of the soul.

It is often through our own darkness that we can find the light, truth, and an expanded awareness. Our own darkness reminds us how strong we are. It awakens an inner knowing and transformation to remember how truly expanded we are and how capable we are.

The mind of heaven embodies within the body. It is empowered in its understanding and truth. It seeks to see others and the world through a higher lens above human judgment and limitation. It sees the world through a higher road and filter. It knows the afterlife is not necessarily after but right within each and every one of us, around us always in all ways.

Chapter Eleven: Surrender to The Light

The cave you fear to enter holds the treasure you seek.
—Joseph Campbell

How would things change if the thousands of transformational experiences—whether they were an out-of-body experience, a shared-death experience, or a near-death experience—were not bogus and were actually right?

Certainly, the old, scientific framework of consciousness produced by the brain is challenged in many ways by all of these experiences. We rationalize that having a healthy brain and still having these bursts of expanded awareness is not explainable. It corners and differentiates the mind as a storage of the filter but not as a producer.

But what if we transformative experiencers were right and tapping into something truthful? How would that change your life?

Plato's allegory of the cave in the *Republic* is something that I often reference when describing NDEs or transformative experiences (the glimpse of reality projected behind them by the powers that be). Once the prisoner breaks free of their shackles, he or she is no longer a prisoner but a free individual with expanded perceptions.

The responsibility and power to be our brothers' and sisters' keepers goes beyond a talking point but rather it becomes a responsibility of truth. It is therefore a goal of transformational experiences to not hold on to these experiences but to share that awakening as something innately inside of each of us.

Being an awakened individual is not something, therefore, in my experience to try to become, as you cannot not be who you truly are as a being made from the same intelligence in the stars, trees, and all things. It is removing all that we are not to embody who we really are.

In the Western society where I grew up, holding is a barrier. We see consciousness as synonymous with our level of awareness. How we view and see ourselves is how we live out our lives. If we have our sole awareness as a physical being, we want to hold on to more physical things. We value possessiveness as a part of our strength and measure sticks of self-worth from diplomas to cars, to kids, to wives. Tangible things become our reality. Once we lose those things outside of ourselves, our identity is then lost.

Surrendering to a higher power is often associated with principles found in recovery orientation in AA. Alcoholics Anonymous has a set of principles that are there to help aid those in recovery. It utilizes a system of twelve steps. One of the hallmarks of AA is within the same principles that saved my own life and self, which is surrender found in the serenity prayer. "With each passing day of our lives, may every one of us sense more deeply the inner meaning of AA's simple prayer:

God, grant US the serenity to accept the things we cannot change,

The courage to change the things we can,

And the wisdom to know the difference."

I tie this principle within life itself and the death and dying process. We cannot change that we are a spiritual being having a finite experience. We cannot change that there is impermanence of the body. What we can change is the ability to know the difference of what we have been taught versus the truth found within.

Many are fearful of the process of letting go, including letting go of the body and letting go of an identity as a partner. It is through letting go that we grow, I have found. If we hold on to who we are and the level of consciousness and worldview that we are operating from, how can we ever grow?

To many, growth is scary. To others, they experience it as necessary. It is life expressing life itself. Many stop themselves out of growth, out of fear of losing, or fear from gaining. As the book *A Course in Miracles* states, "It is not often fear that stops us but our own power."

We have been taught from day one to be small in many ways. From the soul's perspective, the identities that we have to radically accept within our gender, culture, religion, and more are identities but not totalities.

Beyond the temporary hats that we wear is a much greater reality at hand.

To really evolve and come back, many have to stop trying to be what others have told them to be or stop muscling and just embody who they really are. It is often quite liberating to surrender and know the difference between what you have been taught versus what is truly inside of you and to live from that place.

There are a lot of issues within surrender that cause sabotage within the process. The greatest fear that many have is death. From my workshops in doing Past Life Regression or simple meditation, people fear surrendering and letting go. They are afraid they will go crazy or mad. When in reality what led them often to that meditation cushion was holding on to fears.

There is a constant evaluation period that one can benefit from in identifying stale and unproductive comfort zones of consciousness and reality versus uncomfortable healthy zones of growth. Being vulnerable is often a hallmark of growth. Since when were we ever comfortable with a new beginning?

It is new ground, from starting college, to a job change, to a budding relationship. But the reward is great from breaking that period of discomfort. The soul seeks to constantly expand and live out its true freedom. The war outside on this earth is not solved by being at war with each other but by finding peace one soul at a time. This peace starts with developing a closeness with the mind and heart, which are only a couple of inches apart but can feel miles away.

Having the two come into one with the proper foundation of higher awareness, wisdom, and being comfortable with being uncomfortable can lead to quite a productive and rewarding journey. I know from going to the utmost periods of discomfort and suffocation to see the reward in it.

I invite you to do the strongest thing that you have ever done, to unfold yourself to awareness of the power inside of you and around you. Something that saved my life and countless others with addiction through principles of AA is the concept of surrendering our own pain, small self, and lack of control to a greater reality.

This opens us up to remembering our true nature, and that is we were never doing this alone. There is a greater reality at our very fingertips. We just have to be able to lose what we hold on to and break through the shackles of limitation to come to the unencumbered freedom in accepting ourselves as not a body with a soul, but a soul with a body, as Wayne Dyer would say.

Big boys don't cry in sports. Hold it in. "Be a man" and "snap out of it" are all forms of toxic masculinity built into many minds. They come from a place of limitation, fear, and ignorance. Fear of being vulnerable and strong enough to be true to oneself are more than just an image or a body to others. Being empowered and in tune with oneself goes toward a lifetime of honesty to have the strength to challenge different principles of limitation.

This includes the eternal nature of the soul past death, but also speaks to the multidimensional elements of our own being. We were taught to hold on to emotions often and that stoicism is a sign of a strong person. In reality, from my experience, the true strong ones are able to take ownership of themselves and their emotions and reframe the reality that they may have been taught. Truth shall set us free, but the truth is often not found outside of us but within.

Surrendering is powerful as it allows us to be in flow with what is without trying to change or force what is not. One cannot change the fact that their body will die. How do we surrender and have radical acceptance of this? For me, this realization was sped up at a young age. It has led to having an tumultuous early upbringing due to being too wise for my given world.

Later in life, I was able to surrender to a greater truth that the world did not have to create my own mind, but I could surrender into my higher mind, and that could be my own world. Within the human experience, many of us have found a double-edged sword phenomenon of knowing too much. On one hand, it can lead you to feel different, which can be rewarding. Seeing all the large stuff that works others up can seem small from a broader perspective. But it can also lead to a feeling of homesickness, of no longer wanting to be here and wanting to be at home.

The truth is one can never leave home. The light, loved ones, and all beings are forever connected to us. The other side is not, to me, "other" at all, but a part of our reality right here. We merely need to understand that we don't have to die to get to heaven, but we are forever a part of it when the body goes and when we are alive.

One merely has to let go of the limitations of consciousness to set the soul and its inner knowing free. Surrendering does not limit itself as a saving grace for the soul to cross over when the body goes. It also can be helpful for us here in the human experience. I have found that if we believe that everything is in chaos or that we live in a Godless world, we will see more of that. If we believe that life at the end is just and has order, it does not mean that we don't see heartache, pain, or turmoil. We are able to see past it to a bigger reality beyond that pain.

It is important to understand that if we believe there is order, to try to have acceptance and meaning in our very own lives. We can see ourselves as spiritual beings having a human experience, but we must remind ourselves of the order in us being human and to remove the notion that we should not be here.

I know many feel a sense of endless pain, loss, or having no meaning. I like what Viktor Frankl said: "The meaning of life is to give life meaning." I think for all of us it is surrendering to being human and what comes with it while leading our higher awareness to guide us with wisdom, compassion, and mindfulness of this life as an experience but not all that there is.

This engagement with the finite reality and acceptance of it can lead one to see that this is a guided life. A gift. I know I had to understand that from losing my own life to remembering the gift that constantly gives itself even when our bodies have nothing to give. It is about embracing and giving the gift back of finding joy, peace, enlightenment, and meaning. I use the term "find." We can get lost in the hurricane or find the eye of it. In any moment in time, one can recognize that life has very little to do with what is happening on the inside but is eternally existing from the inside.

Our experience and freedom are therefore found in the observer of life and not the absorber. Sadly, many are disconnected from their essence and are lost themselves. Awareness can never be lost, but it can be forgotten. The macro and micro are the same. Sometimes for an individual or a society, a loss of identity that is no longer serving can lead to a greater expansion of consciousness.

My prayer and hope is that one is not living their life from holding on to pain, suffering, and stagnation. But rather, you are empowered, strong in the power of surrender as a force that expands, or aware of the ultimate expansion of life itself. Infinite awareness of our lives as guided, connected, and expanded spiritual beings having this journey in the physical. It separates an awareness from what we eternally are—a spiritual being to this human experience that is temporary.

Many make the mistake by thinking that this is all there is, and that will be a make-or-break position in this world. The moment that you remember who you are and surrender to that truth is the moment that your life will be yours again. The moment that more people in the world remember who we are is the moment that we will shed old paradigms of doing things and find a new birth for a new earth. It is all within the power of letting go.

The globe is having a near-death experience in many ways. My hope is that the world will begin to surrender to the things that do not serve them and evolve to a new awareness based not in the limited story but the unlimited truth inside the doorways of each and every one of us. Surrender and vulnerability are where growth and life begin.

Chapter Twelve: You Are Already What You Are Looking For

Long before I had my near-death experience,
I believed we had to work at being spiritual.
Even after I was diagnosed with cancer I tried
harder to be "spiritual." It was death that made
me realize the truth that I AM spiritual, and
I should not suppress myself in any way!

—Anita Moorjani

I was asked to speak at my dear friend Michael's funeral by his mother after hearing the unwanted news. Michael, for the last few years, had struggled to function as he had a sleep disorder that he could not get past. Despite intervention after intervention, the continual issue was not resolving itself.

He had lost the spark of light within himself that he knew. I tried to be there as much as I could. Given my background as a therapist and being one of his best friends for twenty years, it was difficult to accept the lack of control that I had. After he passed, something his mother said caught my attention: she shared that she believed he had just been surviving all of these years, not living a full life. To be tormented by not getting any sleep was horrible, and he was one of the strongest individuals she knew.

I did my best to understand, though I wasn't quite able to fully put myself in my dear, departed friend's shoes. Instead, I knew I had to embrace the task now given to me: to speak about his life and the goodness that had come from it in front of all his family and friends.

I rushed on a sunny September afternoon through bumper-to-bumper traffic headed into New Jersey. Like many speeches of mine, I didn't really prepare and allowed the doorway of insight and creativity to go beyond my own thoughts and control over what I wanted to say.

I always like to surrender to the moment and let what needs to be said not come from me but through me. I got a text from my brother Gabe while in the car that they were waiting for me. I began to get quite nervous as I was still a few minutes away.

I eventually made my way to the graveside funeral service. Seeing familiar faces and a crowd of suits and dresses with the somber tone stood out in stark contrast with the endless blue sky and sun shining on me. I got up to the podium with Michael's mother nodding at me. I had joked with her the night before when she asked me to speak at her son's funeral. She knew it was hard for me to last five minutes without cursing or saying something inappropriate. Here I was being given a few minutes to sum up over twenty years of friendship.

I took in a deep breath as the crowd braced for what I needed to say. I had a similar feeling of being back in high school given that I felt like a misfit with most of the crowd in their religious garb and living a life from a unidimensional prism of religion. I looked up at the fall sun and thought, *Michael, you were an angel in my life but now I need you to be my archangel. Deliver a tribute for the wonderful soul that you were.*

A flashing image came to mind of the moment when he and I met. It was actually a similar September morning. My mother told me that she had heard of a new boy who had moved to town. She told me that his father was a community rabbi and had recently passed in his sleep. This young man was now beginning to start a new town with his single mother and sister.

The moment I heard his story, I felt as if my soul was on fire, as if it were my calling and responsibility to give this young man a life and take care of him. I remembered shaking his hand and greeting him on a fall Sunday morning over twenty years ago and had an inner knowing that this was a deep soul connection and bond from the start.

The last moment that Michael and I had hung out was at a local amusement park in the Tri-State area. I had often tried to take Michael out, whether it was to baseball games or other events. By then, he was family and I always felt a responsibility to take care of him like a sibling. This time when we got in the car, I noticed a fatigue in him. He mentioned difficulties sleeping. Still, we enjoyed the rides that day, with a feeling of magic in the air.

Now, standing before my friend once more, but this time with his mortal body in the closed coffin, I stepped up to the crowd. Immediately, I had the image of Mitch Albom's great classic book *The Five People You Meet in Heaven.* It had a small Ferris wheel on the cover. To me, that was a perfect allegory and flow to the last time Michael and I spent time together in the flesh. I thought of how the Ferris wheel on Mitch's book summed up the continuity of life; from completion, we begin.

When I began my speech, I glanced up at the sky. The beauty of the first day I met Michael was uniformly of his last day in the physical. Despite all of the difficulty he'd endured during the past few years, he was true to form. I mentioned how he was like the sun to all of us, and that was how I would remember him. Coincidentally, it was September again when the gates of heaven came flying open more than twenty-five years ago when I had my NDE and felt similar, except Michael was returning back home.

Michael's presence had been like a shooting star in all of our lives that came for a bit, but its impact would last. It seems that many powerful spirits that come for a short time in our lives are on such a high level of vibration and evolution that being here in this dense reality can be a challenge; they do not need the amount of years to make an impact. It's as if there is a sense of rush and purpose far greater than the next and an inner knowing of limited time here. Michael came like a meteor to all of us.

I shared with everyone how, on nice days, the two of us would always hang out in my backyard. I mentioned the beautiful trees and the light shining through those moments, as if it felt like I was in an eternal summer. On those peaceful afternoons, something transported us from here to the other side.

I said that I would one day look forward to seeing him in his own backyard. Decades ago, I would go to Michael's nearly every weekend. I would wait outside of the red door of his house in the cold or snow, and he would always be there to greet me. I thought of this life as a microcosm for the other side, knowing that when it was my time to cross over, he and many others would be ready to greet me again.

I left the funeral service with mixed emotions. On one hand, it was overwhelming to go through all of those different waves and emotions. On the other hand, I felt it was never over.

A few months after Michael's passing, I received a dream visitation from him. I entered his house and walked through it on a dreary morning. I expected the same layout of opening up the red door and going up a few steps to a warm kitchen with soft lighting and carpet, ready to be greeted by Michael's big smile, towering figure, and spiked hair.

But this time no one was there, and there was no furniture. It felt quiet, like a pin could drop and sound like thunder. My heart began to feel a sense of emptiness and hollowness in what was a place of home and familiarity for much of my life. I called out and looked through the house, trying to find all of the furniture that had been removed. It felt eerie. I decided to go out the back door, where we spent most of our time shooting hoops or hanging out.

There, by the green grass below beautiful clouds and a shining sun, was Michael with a ball in his hands. He greeted me and motioned for me to come to him and catch. Instantly, memories flew through my mind of when we used to play endlessly in this backyard. Those moments had felt like heaven on earth; this life was not separate from the other side. We could experience it here. That had been our own heaven, via the connections we had, the memories we made, and our ability to transcend experiences in finite moments to infinite bonds.

I had often reflected on Michael and the signs and symbols from his life for readers to understand. I am not a believer in random coincidences; after all, the word comes from the math term "coincide," which means two angles coming together to fit.

I believe that Michael showed me in that dream that the empty house represented the body. When we leave this lifetime, only the body is left. Throughout our lives and even in my speech I mentioned how I wanted to be with him in his backyard one day. I knew even if my body was still alive here, our spirits on one level were always connected.

The backyard represented home and the truth of our essence. I knew this was similar to my NDE I had over twenty-five years ago that transformed a knowing of our truths, wisdom, and eternity that was found within the backyard of us. I had been greeted by an infinite awareness that was deep inside of me and never left me. Houses and bodies come and go. Truth and our essence are forever.

So many moments are filled with chasing what we're looking for. We have been programmed to strive for wisdom versus empowered embodiment. All of what we feel is our essence through material possessions and success eventually dissipates. All that is left is the love, which we need to remember is who we are. We come from a place deep inside of us—of magic, wisdom, insight, and guidance. There is an endless supply of beauty all around us. People stop experiencing the magic when they try to look outside of themselves, lose themselves, and become something to cover over the beauty that they are.

Being connected means living a life from the inside out and from true awareness and foundation of your being. The statement "we are spiritual beings having this human experience" is not a limited talking point but rather a beautiful vantage point to live one's life by. It simply means that when you are true to yourself and live from a deep, foundational place, your whole life will transform.

Seek what is inside of you and not outside, and true transformation will take place. All the things inside last; the things happening on the outside are temporary. This is the embodiment of not just creating heaven on earth but being it.

Looking out for signs and symbols from loved ones is another important skill to develop. As much as we think of them in the afterlife, they also are connected to the lives that we live as well. Our work here is part of their afterlife, so technically just as they are our afterlife, we are, in their eyes, their afterlife too. Our loved ones' languages and senses go beyond the physical senses as they are transformed from form to formless and from finite bodies to infinite consciousness.

Write down different messages you receive that are important. We can only see if we open our eyes and ears beyond the physical. They want to talk; we just have to be willing to let go and listen.

I was truly not going to finish *The Wisdom of Jacob's Ladder.* After Ben's passing, I took time off as I felt lost. My faith wavered when I questioned why such a good soul like my friend was tortured and taken so young. But, thanks to Jeffrey's message he was able to share through his mediumship skills, a spark relit in me.

Sometimes we need to be whacked in the head by Spirit (or, in my case, even get our brains cracked in half to keep us from being in flow and guidance with Spirit). It reminded me that our purpose and connection never end. I know that others on the other side are there with us helping us as our purpose (whether in the body or disembodied) never goes, for our soul's essence is full of divine purpose and meaning.

I thought of the final stage of grief that I often agreed with in transforming the stages to find and experience the meaning of life and a knowing of continuity. It is my hope that through reading this we can truly embody the love inside of us. That love is made to transform life here on earth and move beyond to a calling of healing, purpose, and inspiration.

The soul is never solo. It is here to always be connected and unified. Finding each other is dependent on being there for each other, which leads to unifying each other. Then we can come back home when all things are of the light and there are no sides, but one light connected.

Eternity is a difficult concept to understand within the framework of the finite mind. Here, we are accustomed to beginnings, middles, and endings. There is nothing from this reality that can last forever; it all has a shelf life. But try to ponder that all of us are eternal beings. Beyond this life, there is no end. The creator of this eternity is an infinite, beautiful intelligence far beyond our limited understanding.

How would your life change knowing that, no matter what you do, you will go on? To know the deep essence of life is to know, on a deeper level, God or the creator. Each and every day is an opportunity to live and see the world from a deeper perspective. This is the transformation that goes beyond death as we evolve. So, too, does our afterlife, and so, too, is the eternity that we live in.

Do not be afraid of your own inner power. We were taught that we are synonymous with the story and set characteristics of this lifetime. This is an experience but not the totality of who we are. Beyond this chapter is an endless book. Our stories shift and change with what we choose to write.

You are the author of your own eternity. How you decide to view the world and the given vantage points changes life itself. Living from a deeper essence and seeing glimpses of eternity is a reminder that eternity and the afterlife is not something that we have to wait for: it is actually a place that we can never leave. We only need to see to achieve this awareness.

Let go and allow the soft wind of the doorway of eternity to greet you every day. I promise that you will see and find the afterlife inside of you that always was, is, and will be.

Chapter Thirteen: Question and Answer Section

I have been a fan of the Socratic Q&A for a long time, as both a reader and a presenter. It is a seesaw interview process, where not only does the person asking questions come away with something, but the presenter does as well. In this process, both the teacher and student support each other in a healthy way.

During my many seminars and workshops, I've come across a lot of inquiries, ranging from topics of my own NDE to the subject of higher consciousness. The following section includes the answers to these common questions. I love to invite my readers and the viewers of my workshops to dig deeper into the spirit realm and see things from a broader perspective. The meaning that I find to integrate into my everyday life evolves just as much as I do.

I have included in the following Q&A format handpicked questions that have caught my eye in my presentations from attendees of my work. It is important to note that these answers come from not my limited human experience but through guided higher awareness based on my NDE that helped me back to allowing my mind to be an open channel of wisdom and use it and not allow my mind to use me getting in the way of the higher flow. When I'm looking for solutions to everyday problems, I don't just get answers from myself. I get quiet and know that the question itself and the answer come from two sides of the same coin. Those answers come from a higher consciousness that we are all connected to. This helps me be direct, specific, and share the answers to some big questions in an organized, clear format.

You experienced your NDE at such a young age. How did your age impact your experience?

I learned that through my experience, I did not experience something through my own linear mind and chronological age of my body but its true essence vantage point of the soul. Looking back on it, the soul throughout my life is always there, but the outer representation and integration of the soul within the body and in the lifetime takes time.

I learned as I got older and evolved, the course of events never changed, but my perception of the events in learning how to integrate them helped. Seeing a time when I tried to fit in and had my own death in my teenage years and was empowered to water the seeds of my experience and cultivate once again the angle that I looked at life not from a finite being but an infinite being with this rich experience allowed the lens to change.

I began to look back at the experience as a gift and something that was important to not just ponder, but to process every day so that I could integrate it within my own lifetime and for others. I learned the experience was only as powerful as the displayed portrait and ripple effect to others in finding meaning and a new sense of purpose. I look at the soul the same way as a jewel whose value is reflected on its ability to tap into this realization and shine it to others on their path.

My near-death experience at the age of three put me in a position that contrasted from the conventional development of kids my age. Until that point, like all three-year-olds, I had been learning what it meant to be human, which meant unlearning to be true to my nature as a spiritual being. Then I contracted a severe case of whooping cough. In a moment of suffocation, my body was deprived of oxygen, but my soul was given an eternal breath of wisdom, grace, and clarity. My NDE instantly connected me to the afterlife and changed the trajectory of my human life. I was realigned to my nature as an infinite spiritual being having this human experience. I'll add that this is the true nature of all of us!

My NDE replaced the life blueprint that was being programmed into me with a new one directly from what I refer to as God or source. I was infused with a deep awareness of my nature as an infinite being with a mission to be the god-realization in my interactions. I felt as if God or source was the sun, and my awareness was a panel to transmit its intelligence and wisdom in my everyday actions. When I looked in the mirror, I was no longer seeing just myself within this reality. I was seeing past the ripples of my reflection and recognizing it as part of a greater tapestry. I did not have to wait until I died to see the light but realized that I *was it* and forever connected to it.

As I evolved later on, my NDE motivated me to look at life from the perspective of giving, loving, and serving others through a deeper understanding of God's intelligence as the giver of life. Fortunately for me, my parents already shared these guiding principles. They were devoted to giving. My time volunteering as a teenager with the sick, downtrodden, and vulnerable further demonstrated that life is about caring for all, not just one. It's similar to when one part of the body is injured; you can't ignore the pain just because the rest of the body feels fine.

Healing, not depleting others or the planet for personal gain, became my motive. For me, God or source is the giver of all givers. My work as a psychotherapist is not a man-made construct taught in a classroom but a continuum of a spiritual responsibility that flows from the intelligence of God or source. I am able to transform my craft from the mundane to an expression of the divine within. For me, it's a sacred responsibility.

What assisted you to take ownership of your truth and experience?

I was blessed with many spiritual teachers who spoke to me and my experience. At a young age, I was fortunate to be gifted *Embraced by the Light* by Bettie Eadie. Prior to reading this book, I felt isolated. I couldn't find a way to describe my early experience of connecting through a doorway to the infinite.

Finally, I was able to translate my experience into something a bit more tangible and understandable as well as universal. I understood my wider responsibility to share the gift of my near-death experience with others. I always preface my story by saying I am not the owner.

I am not telling you anything that you don't already know, but hearing "my" experience can bring you back to your personal recollection of the infinite that you are always connected to and someday will be fully aware of again.

How does your experience speak to the current condition and hour of humanity?

As you can imagine, I've pondered many theories about that over the years. Lately I'm recognizing that we are at a delicate time within our existence. The Western world is at a decision point between seeking to self-satisfy or collectively unify through sensitivity and compassion. On one hand, we have access to many practices that open us up to source, consciousness, and higher awareness.

There is mainstream acceptance of yoga, meditation, Reiki, and other modalities. On the other hand, society is filled with increasing tension. I wonder where all of these healing practices are coming into play, because they truly have the power to solve our conflicts. These healing modalities have the potential to translate egocentric perspectives and self-serving impulses into a greater sense of purpose.

Meditation, for example, is not just to make us feel good and be productive but to manage conflict and harmonize with all that is. Much like religion, if we can't separate the forest from the trees and develop a big-picture orientation, things get lost. When we are truly aware that we are one, we are compelled to live it and consider another person's success and well-being as important as our own.

This shift in learning how to work together can be seen as a countercultural practice from day one. Fortunately, it is becoming more acceptable for individuals to recognize that there is more to our personal development than sitting in a classroom, regurgitating information, and learning how to pay the bills.

A deeper part of us seeks and needs more. Professionals within the medical, psychotherapy, and even school systems are becoming aware of meeting not only our basic needs but our soul needs. Just to take a few examples, the drug epidemic and environmental damage makes us ask, just why is it happening and why does it bother us? The "why" will give way to the "how" to fix these problems.

Collectively, we have to decide whether we want to manifest carbon copies of what we've been taught or if we want to integrate our true nature and awareness from another dimension into the earth plane. In the end, love is the only litmus test of success.

What are some ways that people can live in this higher consciousness of love when all that they are around or have been taught is the polar opposite?

The first step is to reflect on how much of our lives is governed by what we learned within our environment. Many have been desensitized to crime and war. Many are defending an insecure identity that is disconnected from others. If what we learned is negative, we may easily create more dysfunctional human "stuff."

But if you think about agents of change like Dr. Martin Luther King, Jr., Rosa Parks, and John Lennon, their achievements would not have been possible if they acted from the vantage point of what they have been taught. Instead, their authenticity came from putting their egos aside to be vessels and channels for truths from a higher dimension. If we operate from a place of serving others, a great value is placed on entrusting the world with insights and examples that go beyond our personal comfort and ease.

Changing the world begins with your understanding of who you are and what you are connected to. Listening to any dissatisfaction within is the first step. Shifting your perspective to that of a spiritual being with higher guiding principles will be a catalyst for yourself and thus the world. This deep authenticity to our true nature creates ripple effects throughout our lives and long after we leave this world.

For those who may not have had a mystical experience or transformative experience, how might they find that inner connection that you experienced, and how do you connect to it on a regular basis?

For me, meditation has been the easiest and most effective way to connect to consciousness and infinite source. Personally, I've found it to be closest to my near-death experience because it is a gentle reminder to release certain thought patterns and stress. The quiet of meditation shows how my true eternal identity is serenity and love.

In the inner world, all is well, and I'm not a prisoner to the fleeting concerns of the outer world. Although something may worry me, it is nothing more than a temporary separation from my truth. I can choose not to give power to something that is outside of that truth. The ultimate reality is that we are infinite spiritual beings capable of connecting to our nature at any moment, no matter what is placed in our path.

Just as most cannot live a day without charging our cell phones or laptops, the same applies to the soul. Meditation is the ultimate tool to recharge and re-center. When I or my clients come to this place of deepened connection, we get in tune with the aspect of our being that I call a sacred observer.

This sacred observer opens us up to wisdom and guidance. The sacred observer points out that whatever unfolds is not random or negative but is *for* us and our growth. I've learned to view life as a school with meditation as study.

Especially for those like me with busy schedules, I have found meditation to be most helpful. Just sitting for a minute or two, being with my breath, and focusing on how I want to feel and experience in the day gets me into focus. The focus is on being, not doing. We get anxious and burn out when we ignore our being and only focus on the doing!

Meditation is reconnecting to the light to remind us of our true nature and to detach from the fear-based world of deadlines and stress. In that reconnection where we realize we are soul beings, not physical beings, our awareness of our responsibilities and requirements changes.

A small shift in perspective has quantum impacts that can improve and even save a life. Breath is sacred, and I had to lose mine to remind myself of this. Don't wait for that moment to appreciate something as sacred, vital, and essential to our living before it is taken from you. Your breath is fuel for your life and unlimited potential.

Is there a proverbial hell on the other side, and did you feel a sense of judgment or disapproval there?

In my NDE, the closest experience I had to hell was when I was in limbo in my body and the spirit realm on the other side. This was a place of pure isolated suffering and pain. The other side, from what I gathered, is not a place that is foreign or separate from us if we don't allow it to be. It is our core at our very essence.

Some throughout life I believe experience hell from forgetting to water their own soul and dwell in their own true living space. I learned that hell doesn't have to happen when we cross over, and I know life can feel like hell from outside experiences, but from an inner perspective, it can happen here on earth. It is hard to truly act kind and good when one is separate from the eternal Light on the other side.

Hell is an overtaking of the human ego and separation of truth from the other side and acting from a false sense of reality and connection. I learned that hell can therefore be a human construct but not a spirit and certainly not a punishment from God. We therefore become our own prisoners and gods based on our actions that align with higher love and truth versus separation.

When one is connected throughout their lifetimes to spiritual principles, light, and love, it is seamless transition. For example, if you never trained for a big race and now are all of a sudden asked to, it is hard to adjust to it.

It has come to my awareness that hell is not a place of punishment but rather an aberration and separation from the truth of the other side. People who dwell in evil have a hard time crossing over as they in their own minds had a different set of rules based on what they thought was right as a separate being rather than eternal principles on the other side. Hell is a separation and difficulty in accepting one's action and a state of limbo and dance between living in darkness instead of letting it go and entering the light.

The life review, I believe, is what holds many spirits back from crossing over, as it is not a place of judgment from God but rather an awareness of a lack of separation between oneself and another. Ultimate reality of us versus them that may have been true on the earth plane is a comical reality.

Therefore, the pain that is inflicted on another becomes the pain and suffering that you experience and feel when going through the review. I do believe dark souls like Hitler, Stalin, and the like are not sent to hell but rather made their own mess to not only others but to themselves as there is no separation on the other side. The darkness created becomes a choice and responsibility to clean up within subsequent lifetimes.

I don't believe a parent punishes their child or thinks that the child is bad when they make a mess. It was an action that they made. Some spend a whole lifetime worthy of making messes, but it does not mean that the person is a mess at their core but rather did not learn the importance of responsibility and ownership and value of taking care of them. Each particular lifetime is an opportunity to shine light on our own shadows.

I look at the life on earth as an allegorical reference to a life that can have darkness around us, and the more that this light shines on the darkness, the more that we don't need heaven the other side for we created it in our own transformation.

Do our guides on the other side ever get angry with us, become judgmental, or give up?

I have learned that guides on the other side is a flexible, evolving process. I do believe that each of us are born with a set guide from the planning phase. Early on in life, there is a pure connection with these guides. Nurturing this relationship and not dismissing it is important. I have learned that guides do not always need to be seen in front of us but can influence our lives in different nudges and ways.

Turning on songs on the radio, having a message that you needed to hear from a friend or even stranger. People in our lives can be channels of guides on the other side. I think it is important to not compare, dismiss, or have one strict rule that many teachers have. I believe everyone's connection to the spirit realm is unique based on each soul, and it is to be validated.

I have come across certain guides whom I have known in the earth plane in my lifetime and those who were there with me before I got into this body who were preordained from the other side. I have understood that guides evolve through their experience. The guides who were there with us on earth might have some of their emotions, judgments, and frustrations with us from the other side. Through guidance, they learn to evolve from these human emotions to love us unconditionally and to be cheerleaders.

In life, we are not necessarily taught what it means to be one with someone and how their success is your success and our success. The other side is a nonstop process of creating unification and evolution among all those in the heavens and earth plane to be closer to this truth. For a closeness to this truth leads to higher levels of closeness to divinity. The more evolved the guide, usually the more patience and acceptance there is.

What do souls do when they are on the other side?

From my NDE, I really learned that there are many levels on the other side. The higher the level, the less overlay humans kind of feel and the more godly and light-filled it was. Beings on the other side, much like us on the other plane, are there to serve and to evolve through their own guidance. They do play and travel. I don't believe that heaven is a true retirement home or resting spot but rather it is quite busy with activities, roles, and duty.

I learned that beings on the other side are there to push and love soul family members on the earth plane to greater heights. There was a great awareness of support and duty to be there through guidance on the other side for loved ones. I believe that loved ones on the other side, while they can travel, are normally with each other on the other side.

Their ties go far deeper that is a spirit pack or ray of God that they are eternally a part of. Much like in life, they can feel like they need a break from this and travel to other dimensions on the other side, but all are connected. This is no different in life that we can go out in our lives on our own felt separate ways but can never truly separate from our identity and home of the infinite light.

What were the major lessons to sum up from your NDE that one can integrate in their everyday life?

I was able to really understand what we are and what we are not. I learned what was a temporary construct through an education here on earth and what was eternal reality principle on the other side. This was the simple message that we are here to love, serve, and remember that we are eternal, tied into each other as one spirit and earth planet.

It is our responsibility to cultivate oneness of this message and remember that we are to always have intuition to understand if the GPS that we are living with is inherited from the earth plane or if it is an eternal principle from the other side. The easiest way to do this is through retreat, reflection, and stopping what we are doing. I had to have this happen to me in the most direct sense in having my life stopping. From this area of stopping and retreat, I was able to propel a life forward. I think it is important to stop and retreat to ask ourselves if we are connecting out of ego or limited awareness, or are we remembering who we truly are.

I learned this lifetime we live is truly temporary and short. I remembered that I was not born here but rather had a purpose that was orchestrated far before I came here. I learned that my life was not a life that was physical or material but rather a way to step past the illusion and use these tools for the spiritual. The physical, spiritual battle that we face is the ultimate measurement of integration of heaven and earth. When the two work with each other, the dissipation of darkness goes away and a magnificent light is cast.

I learned to look at death through the eyes of a cyclical nature. I learned of the karmic and divine order of my NDE and was opened up to a world that I knew I truly belonged to on the other side. I understood from my experience that everything has its time, place, and proper order from the windows of the soul and god's grace that doesn't always register with the linear mind. That linear mind processes events at face value without a deeper understanding of its magnified context. Even what seems to be a struggle often associates itself with endings.

I wasn't afraid of dying in my own body but fearful of others who identified me as my body. I had learned in my travels to the other side that I was much more than that and could not possibly die. I look today at the example of nature, of everything having a season. Going through a forest when looking at a simple tree and seeing its decay below the tree, you can often find sprouts of another tree coming up.

I believe in the cycle of nature as reflective as it relates to passing. From your life, impact, and finishing out a cycle, it is the hope that eternal life can happen on earth from your impact if that is related to ideas, wisdom, and lessons on what to do and what not to do for the next cycle of humanity and their evolution.

What is God, and why does life feel like a series of punishments, injustices, and jail cells to so many purehearted souls?

From my NDE, I learned that God is the highest possible octave, expression, and sensation that you can have. Think of your greatest thought or experience that you have ever had in life, and this does not touch the footsteps of the infinite power of God. God is always in us. It is in the wind that blows in our ears, the oceans that casts their tides, the mountain ridges that splendor in their beauty. It is in all things living and nonliving.

Each lifetime, we are to not only remember heaven but ultimately grow to remember that we are always connected and can never be separated from God. On the earth plane, this realization can be forgotten to us easily by the winds with which we are faced. The most important element is to have a firm and true principle of eternal God that we are not here to be in jail, that there is a reason behind everything.

Dying taught me the true orchestrator of our lifetimes and the intelligence and wisdom within every act that can happen. In the end, we indeed don't die and can never be harmed or punished. We are to remember this and get past the illusion of temporary pain and the realization of eternal love, connection, and support that God is and has for each of us on earth. I believe that when we are truly connected, we are a divine orchestration of the aspect of the divine that we connect to and express.

Learning to forgive life is to let go of temporary moments of suffering and the capacity to understand that which is real can never be taken or removed and that which is temporary has only the legs that hold it up for however long we decide to.

I learned within my NDE that the connection and realization of God did not come from my own brain or own direct analysis on the conceptualization of God but rather through direct experience of the depths of my inner being. I do believe that the soul is an aspect of God, and truly to have an awareness of God, it first starts with having an awareness of soul.

This is easier to do through a feeling sensation rather than learning it. I do believe that we know and have known God since our earliest point of entry as this connects us to our core being. Finding a way to separate with the god of the mind that we have been taught versus the god of the soul through direct experience is helpful.

I learned that God is a personal connection that we all have—an incredibly powerful, unique connection that is eternal. Having my NDE at a young age allowed me to let go of the body, brain, and mind that was being reared to understand a limited God from a limited vantage point of handed-down viewpoints to having a personalized connection with God that no one can take or break from me.

Acknowledgments

They say it takes a village to raise a child. I can attest to this as I was a handful and still can be. I think if that is true, it can take an army of support to help a vision become a reality. I know that it would have been a lot more difficult to write *The Wisdom of Jacob's Ladder* alone.

This is a project that I feel had strong assistance from those in the heavens and here on the earth plane. At times, I wanted to stop writing as I felt the weight of the world. Working full time and then some just became too much. I had reminders from Spirit and those here in my close network of support who never stopped encouraging me to ride out this path.

For all of you and your nudges, I am grateful. I know my name is on this book, but I really see all of your names, handprints, and spirits involved in this dream that is now a reality. I know that it is hard to include everyone in this, and so I thank you all for any part that you had in this project.

Thank you to Mom and Dad. You never stopped believing in me. Your constant follow-up on *The Wisdom of Jacob's Ladder* reminded me to stay on course and move forward with vigor, faith, and conviction. Your relentless pursuits of selflessness, sacrifice, energy, and constantly creating yourself anew have been influential in this project and future aspirations.

Thank you to my wonderful editor, Hannah Lyon, and her powerhouse Castle Lyon Editing. It was great to run it back with you after working with you on my first book. Your talent, sincerity, patience, belief, and understanding are all pivotal on my journey as a developing writer. You have helped a once-remedial college student in writing become a best-selling author. I am humbled and eternally grateful for our teamwork. Behind and with every writer stands a wonderful editor, and we are living proof of this. Thank you also to Katie Connolly and Mallory Campbell. Thank you Carla Green for your beautiful cover design. Thank you William Gladstone and to the entire team at Waterside Productions.

Thank you to my cousin Jane and my Tucson relatives. Thank you, Jane, for your constant unwavering support. A true honor to be your eternal soul family member.

To my dear friend Dr. Sharon Prentice. You never stop making me laugh and think, and you have made me a better writer, person, and teacher. You keep me honest and help see what you see in me and others that you love. Thank you for always being a constant source of unconditional love, support, and inspiration in my life.

Thank you for all of my lifelong friends from day one. You help ground me and see me as Jake as being enough.

Thank you to my friends George Mumford and Edye.

Thank you to my friends and colleagues in the spiritual field. Thank you for always making me laugh and being able to connect with you from the ground up. It's a true pleasure to work by your side and call you friends.

Thank you to all of my media opportunities and endless speaking engagements for giving my writings and teachings a wonderful platform. A special thank you to George Noory from *Coast to Coast AM*, Jeffrey Wands, Max and Mitchell and my friends at KKNW Seattle, Laura Wooster, Allison Dubois, Suzanne Giesemann, Julia Reisler, Sylvia Isachsen, Brian Smith, Marianne Pestana, Jenniffer Weigel, Irene Weinberg, Passion Harvest, Kristy Salisbury, Love Covered Life, Anna Raimondi, The Psychic and The Doc, and countless others for giving a platform and voice to my work on your podcast and radio platforms.

Special thank you to the Forever Family Foundation, Helping Parents Heal, NewLife Expo, The Angel Cooperative, The Crystal Butterfly Boutique, The Eyes of Learning, Molloy College, and The Holistic Center for Soulful Living for hosting me for events.

Thank you to my siblings for your support on my journey. Thank you to my godmother Patti for being an angel through and through in my life. Thank you to all of my uncles, including "The Mailman" for being strong models of influence and support. Thank you to my cousins in Florida and in the Northeast. Special gratitude to my cousin Shari for being a solid rock of support, reasoning, and encouragement.

Thank you to my partner Kari for never giving up hope and always believing in my work and journey and for grounding me when I get too out there. Thank you, Monna Steve, for all of your support.

I have been graced to be influenced by profound spiritual teachers, some with us in the heavens and some here on earth. Special thanks to the late Dr. Wayne Dyer, Sylvia Browne, Thich Nhat Hanh, Fred Rogers, and Kobe Bryant. Endless gratitude to brilliant teachers who never stop putting me in a state in awe. Thank you to my greatest influencers here in the physical: Neale Donald Walsch, Marianne Williamson, Dr. Raymond Moody, Anita Moorjani, and Suzanne Giesmann.

Last but not least, I would like to especially thank one of my greatest sources of wisdom, gratitude, and inspiration in my clients, students, and followers of my teachings. You all inspire me to reach deeper and have a stronger foundation in my teachings. It continually inspires me to seek more solutions when problems arise and dig deeper into the inner fire.

Resources

The following is a list of resources both online and in person that I highly recommend to all my readers. Please read away, do your research, and enjoy the journey.

Books

- *On Death and Dying: What the Dying Have to Teach Doctors, Nurses, Clergy, and Their Own Families* by Elisabeth Kübler-Ross and Ira Byock, MD
- *Finding Meaning: The Sixth Stage of Grief* by David Kessler
- *The Afterlife Frequency* and *Never Letting Go* by Mark Anthony, JD
- *Life to Afterlife - Helping Parents Heal, The Book* by Elizabeth Boisson
- *You Own the Power* by Rosemary Altea
- *Dying to Be Me* by Anita Moorjani
- *Becoming Starlight* by Dr. Sharon Prentice
- *Life After Life* by Dr. Raymond Moody
- *Many Lives, Many Masters* by Dr. Brian Weiss
- *Going Within* by Shirley MacLaine

- *The Gifts Beneath Your Anxiety* by Pat Longo
- *The Mindful Athlete* by George Mumford
- *Gathering at the Doorway* by Camille Dan
- *The Psychic in You* by Jeffrey Wands
- *The Way of the Peaceful Warrior* by Dan Millman
- *Conversations with God* by Neale Donald Walsch
- *Change Your Thoughts, Change Your Life* by Dr. Wayne Dyer
- *The Knowing* by Saje and Serena Dyer Pisoni
- *Journey of Souls* by Dr. Michael Newton
- *Adventures of a Psychic* by Sylvia Browne
- *The Light Between Us* by Laura Lynne Jackson
- *Conversations With Mary* by Anna L. Raimondi
- *Into The Dark* and *Don't Kiss Them Goodbye* by Allison Dubois
- *Messages of Hope* by Suzanne Giesemann
- *Knowing* by Jeffery Olsen
- *Heaven Is Beautiful* by Peter Panagor
- *The Medium Explosion* by Robert Ginsberg

Recommended Mediums/Intuitives

- Glenn Dove: https://www.glenndove.com/
- Gary Joseph: https://beyondthespirits.com/
- Shelby May: https://shelby-may.com/
- Christopher Allen: https://www.imstillhere.net/
- Diane Richards: https://www.dianerichards.net/
- Jeffrey Wands: http://jeffreywands.com/
- Daniel Akner: (631) 836-4205

- Josephine Ghiringhelli: https://josephinege.com/
- Mark Anthony, JD, The Psychic Lawyer: https://www.afterlifefrequency.com/
- Liam Galvin: https://www.liamgalvin.com/
- Gina Simone: https://www.ginasimonemedium.com/
- Sharon Piere: https://sharonpieri.com/
- Laura Wooster: https://laurawooster.com/

Animal Intuitive/Medium

- Susan Allen: https://susanallenmedium.com/about/

Astrologers

- Andrea Mallis: https://www.virgoinservice.com/
- Maria Desimone: https://www.insightfulastrology.com/
- Pauline Southard: https://www.karmickat.com/

Healers

- Pat Longo: https://patlongo.net/new/
- Kimberly Meredith: https://www.thehealingtrilogy.com/
- Yvonne Cook: http://www.wingsoflightandlove.com/

Hypnotherapists

- Carol Denicker: https://newyorkhypnosistrainingcenter.com/carol-denicker/
- Kathie Lapinksi: https://kathielipinski.com/

Grief Support/Counseling Services

- Forever Family Foundation: https://www.foreverfamilyfoundation.org/
- Helping Parents Heal: https://www.helpingparentsheal.org/
- Dr. Amy Olshever: https://amyolshever.com/
- Katrina Michelle, PhD, LCSW: http://www.thecuriousspirit.org
- Elisabeth Kübler-Ross Foundation: https://www.ekrfoundation.org/
- David Kessler: https://grief.com/

Suicide Hotline

National Suicide Prevention Hotline: (800) 273-8255

Recovery/LGBTQ Support

- The Holistic Center for Soulful Living: https://soulfullivingcenter.com/
- The Trevor Project: https://www.thetrevorproject.org/
- Other Mental Health Services: Please check referrals under *Psychology Today* or contact your insurance companies. www.psychologytoday.com

Recommended Shows

- *Surviving Death,* Netflix
- *Heal* documentary, Netflix
- *Unexplained Mysteries,* Netlix

Cancer Support

- Adelphi University Breast Cancer Hotline and support group: https://breast-cancer.adelphi.edu/

Mindfulness

- George Mumford: https://georgemumford.com/

Jacob's Ladder Citations

- According to Dr. Gabor Maté, renowned specialist in anxiety and addiction, the "difference between passion and addiction is that between a divine spark and a flame that incinerates."
  - *In the Realm of Hungry Ghosts*, page 116

- As psychologist Carl Jung wrote, "Loneliness does not come from having no people about one, but from being unable to communicate the things that seem important to oneself."
  - *Memories of Dreams and Reflections*, page 356

- To quote Ram Dass, "Our whole spiritual transformation brings us to the point where we realize that in our own being, we are enough."
  - *Be Here Now*

- A profound teaching from Annie Kagen in her book The Afterlife of Billy Fingers is, "if there is one thing worth living on the planet it is discovering self-love."
  - *The Afterlife of Billy Fingers*, page 75

- Now, remember one of the most important parts: the same applies to the self. As Marianne Williamson says in her book Return to Love, people can be mean, but we can be vicious toward ourselves.
    - o *Return to Love*, page 6

- As Buddhist teacher Pema Chödrön said, "Nothing ever goes away until it has taught us what we need to know."
    - o *When Things Fall Apart*, page 66

- Clinical Psychiatrist, Dr. Brian L. Weiss, a pioneer of Past Life Regression, wrote that "without understanding, patterns tend to repeat, unnecessarily damaging the relationship."
    - o *Messages from the Masters*, page 68

- As Wayne Dyer said, "When you judge another, you do not define them, you define yourself."
    - o *Ten Secrets for Success and Inner Peace*, page 63 (e-book)

- As Wayne Dyer wrote, "Heaven on Earth is a choice you must make, not a place you must find."
    - o *Co-Creating at its Best: A Conversation Between Master Teachers*, by Dr. Wayne Dyer and Esther Hicks

    "Humans often think that this is just a trial ground and that Heaven is where it's at. But this is the Leading Edge of thought. This is where the thought manifests. This is where it is at. Earth is crammed with Heaven. Earth is Heaven."

- There are two phrases from famous Swiss psychiatrist and renowned psychoanalyst Carl Jung that I love. In his reference to the stages of life, he said, "Thoroughly unprepared, we take the step into the afternoon of life. Worse still, we take this step with the false presupposition that our truths and our ideals will serve us as hitherto. But we cannot live the afternoon of life according to the program of life's morning, for what was great in the morning will be little at evening and what in the morning was true, at evening will have become a lie."
    - o *Modern Man in Search of a Soul*, page 108 or page 111

- I love how my good friend and author of *The Mindful Athlete* George Mumford often says, "If you do not know who you are you can be anybody. and if you do not know where you are going you can be anywhere."
    - o Personal quote

- Echart Tolle, the best-selling author of *The Power of Now* said it best: "Death is a stripping away of all that is not you. The secret of life is to 'die before you die'...And find that there is no death."
    - o *The Power of Now*, page 46

- Rumi the Sufi poet stated, "From the moment you came into this world, a ladder was placed in front of you that you might transcend it."
  - o *A Garden Beyond Paradise: Love Poems of Rumi,* by Jonathan Star and Shahram Shiva, page 148

  "From the moment you came into this world, a ladder was placed in front of you that you might escape. From earth you became plant, from plant you became animal. Afterwards you became a human being, endowed with knowledge, intellect, and faith."

  (Improper punctuation because the quote is written as prose.)

- According to studies, suicide is the tenth leading cause of death and each year there are one million suicides. Every forty seconds, a suicide is recorded.

- I was deeply taken by the writings of philosopher Albert Camus. One statement that he made that really speaks to eternal awareness of the summer within any moment is referenced by this: "In the midst of winter, I found there was, within me, an invincible summer.

  "And that makes me happy. For it says that no matter how hard the world pushes against me, within me, there's something stronger—something better, pushing right back."

("Return to Tipasa" from *The Myth of Sisyphus, Personal Writings, The Stranger,* or *Summer*)

- o *Personal Writings,* page 182
  "In the depths of winter, I finally learned that within me there lay an invincible summer."
  (The second part of the quote can be found in *Summer,* 1954)

About the Author

Based on his near-death experience and past life regressions, Jacob L. Cooper, LCSW, shares insight about the mystery of life on the other side of the veil. In addition to peace and euphoria in the afterlife, we also experience these feelings in the physical world; there is so much more to live for, as we are much more resilient than we imagine. Jacob's experience provides the guidance for others to experience past-life memories by assisting in the development of self-awareness and finding meaning in their experiences.

Jacob holds a master of social work (MSW) degree and is a licensed clinical social worker, certified Reiki master, certified hypnotherapist, and specializes in Past Life Regression Therapy. As a psychotherapist, Jacob works with individuals, groups, and families to uncover emotional barriers, promote improved wellness, and achieve resiliency. Jacob incorporates mindfulness and a spiritual approach to focus on the connection between the mind, body, and spirit. In effect, this teaches individuals how to improve cognitive processing and shift their perspective.

Jacob is a sought-after speaker on grief, wisdom, and consciousness and offers meditation and mindfulness seminars to individuals and groups, many of whom have been diagnosed with cancer, developmental disabilities, and those experiencing symptoms of aging. Jacob has presented at the Edgar Cayce Association for Research and Enlightenment (ARE), the International Association of Near-Death Studies (IANDS), the Forever Family Foundation, spiritual centers, international universities, and public libraries.

Jacob's seminars promote healing for those grieving, people who seek to understand continuity of consciousness beyond the physical body, and those with anxiety associated with the fear of life after death. He is the author of *Life After Breath*, a memoir about his near-death experience published by Waterside Productions, with literary agent William Gladstone. Jacob resides and practices in Long Island, New York.

Also by Jacob Cooper

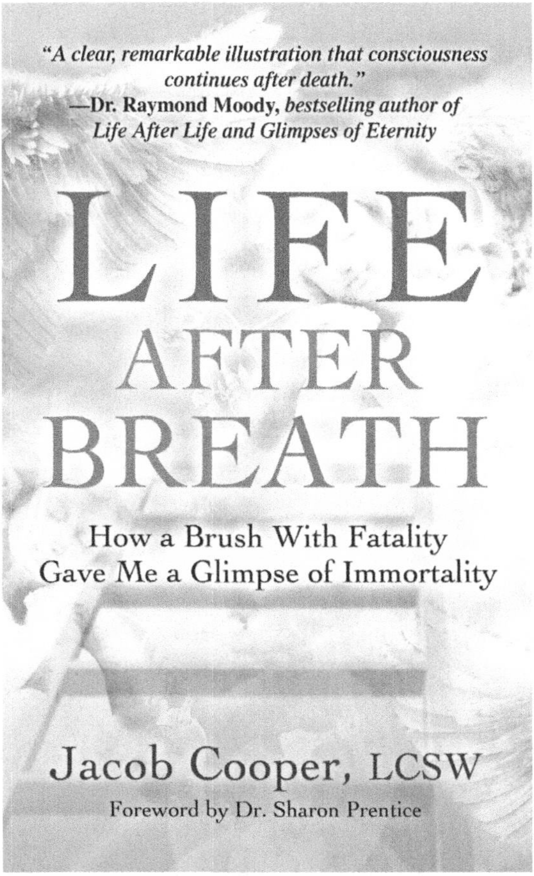
"A clear, remarkable illustration that consciousness continues after death."
—Dr. Raymond Moody, bestselling author of Life After Life and Glimpses of Eternity
LIFE AFTER BREATH
How a Brush With Fatality Gave Me a Glimpse of Immortality
Jacob Cooper, LCSW
Foreword by Dr. Sharon Prentice